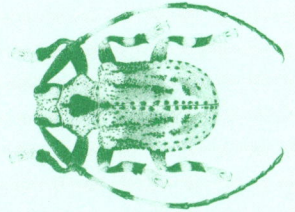

THE WONDER
OF INSECTS

First published in Great Britain in 2025 by Laurence King, an imprint of The Orion Publishing Group Ltd, Carmelite House, 50 Victoria Embankment, London EC4Y 0DZ

An Hachette UK Company

The authorized representative in the EEA is Hachette Ireland, 8 Castlecourt Centre, Dublin 15, D15 XTP3, Ireland (email: info@hbgi.ie)

10 9 8 7 6 5 4 3 2 1

A CIP catalogue record for this book is available from the British Library.

ISBN (Hardback) 978 1 39962 571 5
ISBN (eBook) 978 1 39962 572 2

Commissioning Editor: Tina Persaud
Senior Editor: Katherine Pitt
Art Director: Liam Relph
Design: Hannah Beatrice Owens
Production: Sarah Cook
Origination by f1 colour Ltd
Printed in China by C&C Offset Printing Co., Ltd

Front and back covers: Carim Nahaboo

MIX
Paper | Supporting responsible forestry
FSC
www.fsc.org   FSC® C104740

www.laurenceking.com
www.orionbooks.co.uk

THE WONDER OF

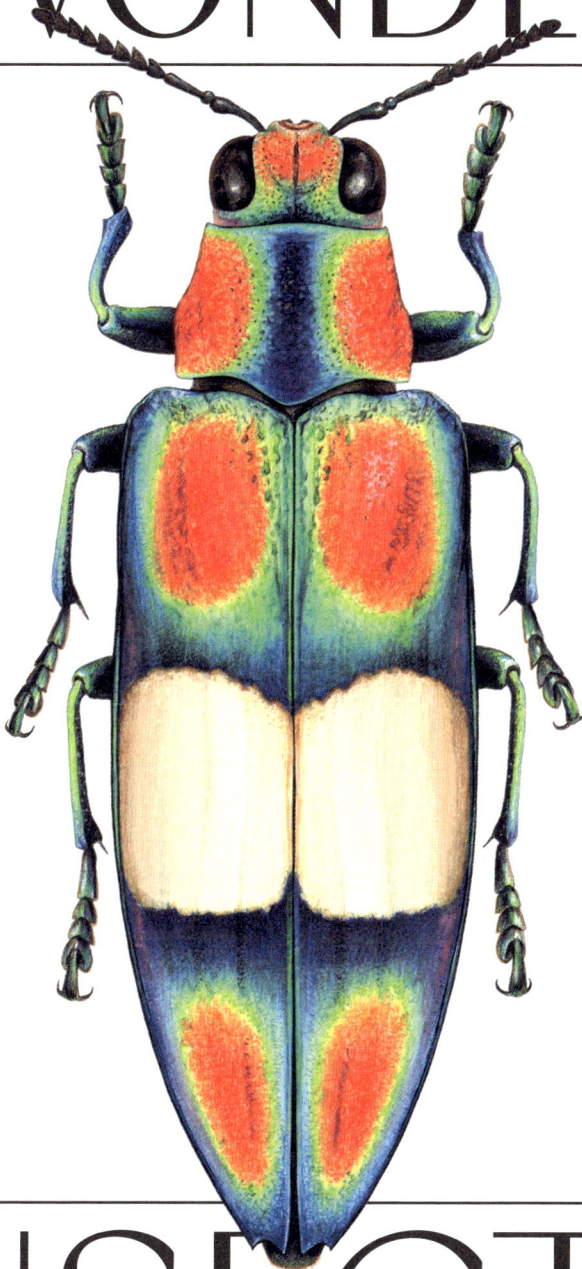

INSECTS

DR. ROSS PIPER

CONTENTS

INTRODUCTION

've been fascinated by insects for as long as I can remember. It's their sheer diversity that does it for me – just over one million species, with millions more still out there and so much still to learn about their biology. Among the animals they are completely unparalleled in terms of species number and the breadth of their lifestyles, from spindly, blind cave dwellers to disc-shaped, sucker-cup-equipped larvae that only inhabit waterfalls and aerial beings of superb skill and flair, some of which migrate huge distances on the wing.

With so many species and individuals, they have their feet in a lot of pies, ecologically speaking. Whether it's pollination, the recycling of organic matter, the churning of the soil or simply being eaten by larger animals, their reach is immense. Without them, ecosystems that support our food supply would collapse, and humans wouldn't survive very long at all.

The purpose of this book is to give you a flavour of insect diversity. We delve into the biology and cultural significance of 70 remarkable species, grouped by size, shape, colour and pattern. I have also drawn on my experiences watching and pursuing insects, which has taken me to some remarkable places, from the deserts of Namibia to the forests of northern Myanmar. Hopefully, what you read and see here will make you want to go and find out more. Hone your powers of observation and you'll be amazed at what you can find, even on your own doorstep.

The backstory

To better appreciate the diversity of the insects we see around us today, we need to know a bit about where they came from. Their story goes back a very, very long way with their likely origins at least 480 million years ago, when their ancient ancestors – marine crustaceans – began exploring the terrestrial frontier. They were hot on the heels of the first plants that were already greening the margins of the seas, steadily edging further inland. Between then and now, the Earth has been many different worlds, but the insects took to a life on land and made it their own, colonizing just about every terrestrial and freshwater niche, and surviving a number of mass extinctions. Not only were they among the pioneers of the land, but they were also the trailblazers of the air, taking flight at least 170 million years before any vertebrate got off the ground.

Set up for success

Why are the insects so successful? This is a good question, the answer to which is rooted in their body plan. Firstly, their skeleton – the exoskeleton – is on the outside. Not only does this provide all of the attachments for the insect's muscles, but it also prevents water loss – pretty important for any self-respecting land dweller. Time and natural selection have moulded the exoskeleton into myriad appendages, from the delicate straw-like mouthparts of the mosquitoes to the shovel-like front legs of Mole Crickets and the elaborate wings of Moon Moths. The exoskeleton does have some limitations, namely that it doesn't stretch, so must be periodically shed in order to grow, but this is the merest inconvenience given its many strengths.

Perhaps the most transformative innovation in the insect success story was the evolution of wings and the ability to fly. Fine-tuning the wings and their muscula-ture opened up all sorts of possibilities. Flight enabled insects to better evade their enemies, to hunt prey and to seek out mates and new areas of habitat. The ability to fly long distances is not something we normally attribute to the insects, but lots of butterflies, moths, hoverflies, beetles and many more insects undertake enormous migrations every year.

Moving through the air at speed and covering more ground also spurred sensory refinement and innovation. The insects alive today have a suite of complex senses that belie their small size. There are mechanoreceptors on the surface and within their body which sense stretching, bending, compression and vibration. Many of these are used to sense the environment, such as the minuscule movements of air which might indicate the proximity of prey or predators, while others provide information on the position/orientation of the body. In some beetles and true bugs, mechanoreceptors have even been modified to detect the infrared from forest fires. Seeking out raging infernos might not seem like a sensible strategy, but the offspring of these insects can only develop in the wood of burnt trees, so they've evolved these remarkable heat sensors.

Hearing in insects normally involves receptors that pick up the tiniest vibrations travelling through the substrate, but some insects, like mammals, detect movements of the air via a drum-like membrane, which gives them among the sharpest hearing in the animal world. The ability to detect chemicals – i.e. taste and smell – is extremely acute in insects. These senses are normally concentrated on the mouth-parts, but they can also be found on the antennae of many insects as well as on the feet and ovipositor of others. The life cycle of many insects hinges on being able to detect mates and food from afar, so their ability to sense individual molecules in the air is remarkable.

Insects are often furnished with two types of eye: simple eyes and compound eyes. Simple eyes detect light levels and can also adjust the sensitivity of the compound eyes, which can be relatively enormous and are made up of individual, tightly packed units. Each of these units captures an image that is relayed to the brain. Up until very recently, it was assumed compound eye vision was rather low resolution, but it turns out the light-sensitive cells in these eyes move rapidly and automatically in and out of focus, which provides a view of the world that is much sharper than previously thought. As well as giving insects a sharp view of the world, these compound eyes also have a very wide angle of view and are second to none when it comes to detecting movement. Most insects can also see parts of the colour spectrum that are invisible to us, e.g. ultraviolet light.

Dealing with the rush of sensory information that came with whizzing around in the air and navigating complex habitats, required more powerful brains, which are at their most sophisticated in insects such as social wasps and bees. Imagine being one of these animals. Tasked with foraging, you have to find food in the big, bad, complex world. This might mean flying several kilometres from the nest; that's like us having to travel hundreds of kilometres to the supermarket. You find some food and then have to navigate your way back. Once back at the nest, you have to tell your sisters all about it. The brains of social insects have to cope with a lot of information and formulate the correct response. As well as lots of innate 'hard-wired' behaviours, these and many other insects can actually learn. Social wasps can recognize the faces of other wasps, while honeybees can count, discern if two symbols are different and even teach their sisters about the location of food, water and new nesting spots using symbolic language. Are they intelligent? Certainly, but our language and the framework we have for understanding intelligence is geared towards us and a few other vertebrates. The 'otherness' of insects clouds our understanding.

All of this biological complexity is squeezed into a tiny space – the insects embracing miniaturization like few other animals. Compared with a big body, a small body is 'cheaper' to produce and maintain, especially in terms of the various systems that are needed to get around the problems of ventilation, nutrient distribution and excretion. Small animals can also exploit niches that are completely inaccessible to larger animals. In addition, the capacity to exploit all sorts of niches is enhanced by the ability of most insects to undergo a radical transformation during their development. This process of metamorphosis has captivated people for thousands of years and it is another reason why these animals are so successful. The most diverse groups of insects – the beetles, flies, wasps, bees, ants, butterflies and moths – all go through metamorphosis. A separate larval stage and adult stage allow a division of labour in the life of an insect. The larval stage is an eating machine – dedicated solely to growth, while the adult gets all the fun and can spend its time mating and finding new areas of habitat. The other master stroke of this strategy is that because the larva and adult are so different and typically live in different places they won't compete for resources.

As a rule, insects are very good at making more insects, with legendary fecundity and a rate of development that makes rodents look like career-minded professionals. Take the humble Cabbage Aphid, an animal capable of knocking out 41 generations in a single season. If all of these survived, we're talking about 600 billion offspring from a single aphid in a single season. The super-charged reproduction of aphids and some other insects is because they do away with males for some or all of their life cycle. The females churn out copies of themselves. Perhaps the most important aspect of this rampant reproduction is that it cranks out mutations, a tiny proportion of which will be beneficial and allow the owners to adapt to a continually changing world.

Challenging times

Regardless of how successful they are, insects face a new challenge in the shape of us. Long-term data from lots of places around the world appear to show that some insects are in steep decline – a direct result of human activity. We've been very good at making more humans, our growing population bending more and more of the environment to our needs. The destruction and fragmentation of habitats, as well as pollution, especially pesticides, wipes out populations and species, leaving any survivors isolated and vulnerable to other calamities.

Many insect species are also threatened by climate change. Not only do rising temperatures reduce the fertility of male insects, but they also alter entire ecosystems, mess with the seasons and force species to move to stay within their preferred temperature range.

We've also lit up the world, our artificial lighting disrupting the normal behaviour of nocturnal insects. There's even evidence to suggest that our wireless communication technologies and electricity transmission infrastructure might be frazzling insects and disrupting their ability to navigate through the landscape.

Still, with all the challenges they face, we must remember that insects are nothing if not resilient. They've been around for a very long time, coming through the various cataclysms that have wiped out trilobites, ammonites, non-avian dinosaurs and lots more besides. The environmental damage wrought by the overreach of the human species is undoubtedly reducing insect diversity and will continue to do so unless we change course. What about the long term and far into the future though: 10,000 years ... 100,000 years ... one million years? Insects will undoubtedly rebound from whatever we've inflicted on them. As long as there's an Earth, there will be insects. Who knows, far into the future they might even get a crack of the whip, giving rise to an intelligent civilization. Now there's a thought ...

COLOUR

BLUE MORPHO

Against a backdrop of verdant greenery flies a Blue Morpho (*Morpho cypris*), its undulating, frenetic flight revealing fleeting glimpses of the striking, iridescent-blue upper wings. With a wingspan of more than 10 cm, this is a stunning butterfly. Seeing one in any setting is quite something, but watching them in flight in the wild is a quintessential Neotropical experience.

The glorious shimmering blue of the upper wings changes depending on the angle at which it is viewed. No blue pigments are at work here. Rather, what we see is an example of structural colour. Look closely at the wing and you'll see it's covered in what looks like dust. This 'dust' is actually tiny scales, each of which is the flattened outgrowth of a single cell. Overlapping like miniature roof tiles, these scales are a mere 0.2 mm long and 0.07 mm wide. It is these scales that give butterfly and moth wings their colours and patterns.

Now, if you had a scanning electron microscope handy, you would see that the tiny scales of the Blue Morpho wing are far from just boring, flat structures. You would see slits formed by grooved ridges that look in cross section like stylized Christmas trees. The distance between these slits is about half the wavelength of blue light, so the blue light enters these slits and pings around the grooves and is eventually reflected, interfering with the incoming light as it does so. This is known as constructive interference, and it results in the blue light being boosted and enhanced as the shimmering iridescence we see. Other wavelengths of visible light are not reflected, hence why we only see the blue.

What benefit does the butterfly gain from having shimmering blue wings? We're not entirely sure, but it may help them to evade their main predators – birds. With each flap of their wing, there's a flash of blue and as the wings are folded in preparation for the downstroke the butterfly is momentarily much less conspicuous, blending into the background. Combine this with their energetic, erratic flight and they are very hard to track. Believe me, catching one is extremely difficult. Unlike us, birds can see ultraviolet (UV) light, and the iridescence and colour of the Morpho's wings may be even more intense when seen in UV. This probably enhances the dazzle and momentary 'disappearance' of the butterfly in flight.

When at rest, only the underside of the Blue Morpho's wings is visible. The muted colours of this surface, coupled with large eyespots, help them to blend in when perched on a branch or tree trunk.

Among the most striking butterflies, Blue Morphos have become a regular sight in butterfly houses, requiring a steady supply of eggs, caterpillars and pupae from the tropical forests where they are found. In some cases, these may be wild caught, which is bad news for them and the forests. However, there are growing numbers of butterfly farms in tropical areas that help to protect forests and provide locals with an alternative livelihood.

Actual size

EPOMIS

Being rather small animals, insects are nearer the base of the food chain than the top, meaning they are on the menu for a huge range of other animals. There is a wide variety of vertebrates that specialize in eating only insects – just think of all the insectivorous bird and mammal species, not to mention all the other species that make short work of insects whenever the opportunity arises.

Of course, I understand that insects do have their place, but it is cause for celebration when they turn the tables on these larger animals – when prey becomes predator. This is extremely unusual and there are very few examples of insects predating vertebrates. Large aquatic beetle larvae and bugs (see page 69 – Giant Water Bug) do routinely catch and eat fish and amphibians. There are even documented cases of dragonflies predating small hummingbirds, but this is exceptional. In these cases, though, the insects in question are the same size, even larger than the unfortunate vertebrates in question.

One of the most remarkable cases of an insect turning the tables on a vertebrate – a real David and Goliath story – is that of the *Epomis* beetles, the larvae of which tackle prey way larger than themselves – frogs and toads to be exact.

Epomis larvae are purposeful-looking characters with outsize heads bearing enormous, recurved mandibles which bend back towards their bodies. They're even adept at luring their victims, waving their mouthparts and antennae, mimicking the movement of the small prey these amphibians find irresistible. A curious frog comes to investigate, eventually making an open-mouthed lunge at what it thinks is an easy snack. It initially swallows the *Epomis* larva, but this is a mistake and something to be quickly regretted. Being swallowed, although seemingly risky, is all part of the beetle's ploy. Try as the frog might to swallow what looked like a tasty morsel, the *Epomis* larva uses its grappling hook mandibles to latch in the frog's throat.

There's little the frog can do now. The larva might start to feed on the hapless victim from the inside, although, utterly appalled by what it has just attempted to eat, the frog can also regurgitate the beetle larva. This just prolongs the struggle because the larva changes its grip and latches onto the underside of the frog's head. The demise of the frog is fairly quick, perhaps hastened by substances in the larva's saliva. For such a soft-bodied animal, the *Epomis* larva is incredibly tough, surviving being swallowed and then regurgitated before feeding at leisure on the incapacitated amphibian.

Even adult *Epomis* beetles are partial to the odd frog or toad, but they are opportunists, attacking them from the rear and biting them in the hindquarters to paralyse the legs. Unable to flee, the frog is consumed by the beetle.

JEWEL WASP

J ewel Wasps (*Chrysididae*) are an object lesson in just how beautiful and complex insects are when we take the time to really look at them. The common name of these wasps is richly deserved as many of them sport a rainbow of sparkling iridescent colours. This is another example of structural colouration (see Blue Morpho on page 14) where microscopic structures in the exoskeleton reflect specific wavelengths of light.

The reasons why these wasps should have an embarrassment of riches in the structural colouration department is not fully understood. Most of them are extremely active, fast-moving insects, flitting around the nests of their hosts and nectaring on flowers. It's possible the shimmering hues and patterns are a form of camouflage – protection against sharp-eyed birds. Wasps are active in bright sunlight and rarely keep still for long and the structural colouration may render them fleetingly invisible to a bird. In addition to the colours, the exoskeleton of these wasps is richly sculptured with dimples. The function of these is a mystery. They might add to the structural colouration somehow, improve aerodynamics or simply be a consequence of a thick, layered exoskeleton.

If this dazzling display is a form of camouflage, it's of precious little use where they need it most though – to avoid detection in the nests of their hosts. The other common name for these insects is Cuckoo Wasps. Again, this name is well deserved because they surreptitiously enter the nests of other wasp and bee species to destroy the nest-maker's egg(s) before laying their own. The Jewel Wasp's offspring will gorge on the provisions diligently stocked by the nest maker.

If they're caught in the middle of this heinous act by the nest maker, they're in trouble. They could try and make a sharp exit, but it's more likely that a fight would ensue which could easily end in a bit of a figurative bruising, even death. The extremely tough exoskeleton of the Jewel Wasp affords it some protection from the jaws and sting of a maternally enraged host, and it can even roll into a ball to present the very toughest parts of its armour to the attacker.

Avoiding a confrontation altogether would be much more sensible and at least one species of Jewel Wasp has a secret weapon that allows it to do just this. The nests that this particular Jewel Wasp species must enter belong to the Beewolf (page 118). These nests are underground and therefore pitch-black, so apart from literally stumbling upon them the only sense the host can rely on to detect the intruder is smell. The interloper has a chemical cloak though – its odour mimics that of the host, so it can prowl the subterranean brood chambers largely immune to detection.

As very visual beings, we often completely overlook this aspect of nature. In addition to bright colours and patterns, insects use complex cocktails of odours to communicate and deceive. The ability of this Jewel Wasp to mimic the odour of its host for nefarious purposes hints at the extraordinary interactions that take place all around us in the natural world, most of which remain to be deciphered.

BONE-SKIPPER FLY

This is one distinctive fly, what with its bright orange head and metallic blue body and legs. It's so distinctive that entomologists couldn't find it for more than 150 years.

To be fair, not all that many people were looking for it, and its habits are, shall we say, interesting – certainly unsavoury and specific enough to have put off casual observers who might otherwise have spotted it. You see, these flies (*Thyreophora cynophila*), are completely dependent on large mammal carcasses, such as those of deer, boar, dogs, sheep, cows and horses. To make life even more of a challenge for themselves, the larvae of these flies like to feed on marrow from within the long bones and spine of these carcasses. This is quite some niche.

Originally described in 1798, after a specimen was found in Mannheim, Germany on a dead dog (hardcore entomologists like nothing more than rooting around in dried carcasses), the species turned up a few times until 1850. It wasn't seen again until 2007, when some entomologists working near Madrid in Spain found six of them in their pitfall traps which had been baited with moreish, rancid squid.

Between 1850 and 2007, this fly acquired almost mythical status – well, among some entomologists. Things actually got a bit weird in the long hiatus and bold claims were made about it. For example, Carl Robert Osten-Sacken, a Russian diplomat and entomologist, claimed the fly's orange head emitted a luminous shine. This was utter garbage, but this strange fly obviously loomed large in the imagination of fly-fanciers who had never actually seen it.

Since its rediscovery, this fly has turned out to be rather abundant in Spain and it has also been found in France. Why, then, did it evade entomologists for so long? I've already touched on the rather specific and off-putting habitat requirements, but it also turns out the adults are only to be found between January and March, the cold months

Between 1850 and 2007, this fly acquired almost mythical status.

when nearly all entomologists are holed up in their dens, putting specimens to the pin, dreaming of balmier weather. To add still further to their elusiveness, the flies are normally active at night. So, the long absence of this species is more about the dire shortage of fly-fanciers who like ferreting about in foetid carcasses at night … in the winter.

Even though this fly is alive and well in Spain and France, it hasn't been seen in the places where it was originally encountered. There has been a trend over time to tidy up the countryside. Laws were passed and large, dead animals had to be properly disposed of, depriving the Bone-skipper Fly and a whole raft of other species of food and a place to live. The eradication of wolves from much of Europe also made things difficult for this creature. Wolves are able to crack the large bones of ungulates, affording the entry of the fly larvae into the marrow cavity where they feed and grow fat. With the return of wolves to many of their old haunts, an enlightened attitude towards tidiness in the countryside and recognition of the importance of nature's recyclers, this fly may soon be coming to a carcass near you.

BONE-SKIPPER FLY

This winter-active fly relies on the carcasses of large mammals and was thought to be long extinct, until its rediscovery in 2007.

LITHINUS RUFOPENICILLATUS ├─────────────────────┤ MADAGASCAR

MOSS WEEVIL

Rolling stones gather no moss, but what about ambling weevils? It turns out that at least one of them not only gathers moss, but actually cultivates a moss garden on its back. In what is a living ghillie suit, this Madagascan beetle is practically invisible on moss-covered branches. The Moss Weevil (*Lithinus rufopenicillatus*) and its close relatives are characterized by a rough, bristly upper surface, which breaks up their outline admirably and allows them to blend in on lichen-covered branches and other such places. In this particular species, the roughness and the bristles create ideal conditions for mosses and other tiny plants to colonize and thrive. Perhaps they also lack the oils that other species produce to prevent debris and living things from adhering to their exoskeleton. Cultivating this moss garden also takes time, so by typical insect standards these are long-lived – the adults milling about and pretending to be bits of moss for three years or more.

Camouflage is something that insects are rather good at. They have to be because a huge variety of larger animals want to eat them, but the Moss Weevil is in a league of its own because what actually provides the camouflage is other living things – the mosses in its garden. This is Madagascar we're talking about though, a place where the 'Go home, evolution, you're drunk' meme applies to so many of its unique denizens.

To understand what makes Madagascar such a treasure trove of biodiversity, we need to look to the deep past. Long ago, there was a supercontinent called Pangea, which fractured into a northern landmass, Laurasia, and a southern one, Gondwana. What we know today as Antarctica, Madagascar, the Indian subcontinent and Australasia made up the eastern part of this southern landmass, which would also be wrenched apart by the slow, inexorable churning of the Earth's mantle. About 90 million years ago, Madagascar finally split from the continental plates bearing the Indian subcontinent and the Seychelles, and its inhabitants continued to evolve in glorious isolation. Today, around 90% of Madagascar's animal and plant species are found nowhere else. Alas, their uniqueness has afforded them little protection, with humans doing a pretty thorough job of denuding this enormous island of its forests, destroying the habitats of countless species.

Still, there is a lot to fight for. Between 1999 and 2010, scientists discovered 615 new species in Madagascar, and, like so many other places, this is the tip of the veritable iceberg. Insects like this weevil, beautifully camouflaged by its moss garden, are very easily overlooked, so just pause to reflect on what other wonders are still to be discovered on this great evolutionary experiment in the Indian Ocean.

MOPANE WORM

The idea of eating insects is one that is generally met with revulsion in Western countries, which is strange when you think about it. We greedily scarf a panoply of crustaceans, including prawns, lobsters and crabs, and yet insects – the terrestrial brethren of these marine animals – turn many of us right off. Things are, however, beginning to change as the many benefits of eating insects become clear. Not only are they packed with protein, fats, vitamins and minerals, but rearing them is wonderfully efficient; producing a kilogram of insect protein requires much less land, water and feed and produces much less greenhouse gas than a kilo of cow, sheep, pig or chicken protein.

Many insect species also thrive on what we would normally just throw away, turning domestic and industrial food waste into high-quality food. It's a win-win situation that is the basis for numerous companies across Europe which produce Black Soldier Flies, the larvae of which consume food waste. By 2033, these companies are expected to produce a whopping 4.6 million tonnes of these fly larvae annually, worth $2.3 billion. Currently, most of these fly larvae end up as insect meal that is used as high-quality feed in agriculture and aquaculture, reducing the need for increasingly expensive and environmentally damaging alternatives, such as soy and fish meal. It won't be long, though, before we're happily tucking into all sorts of products made with insect meal.

In many parts of the world, insects have been on the menu for as long as there have been people. One of the most well known of these edible insects is the Mopane Worm (*Gonimbrasia belina*), which is not a worm at all, but the colourful caterpillar of a type of Emperor Moth. In southern Africa, these caterpillars, known locally as *madora* and *amacimbi* among other names, are an extremely valuable source of protein, containing three times more than beef – and also offering iron, zinc and fibre. They are harvested in their millions each year. The leaves of the mopane tree are the favoured food of the caterpillars, from which they are hand-picked or shaken, mostly by women who can collect 25 to 50 kg of them per day. Once the caterpillars are harvested, the back end of each is pinched, squeezing out the unpleasant-tasting organs and part-digested leaves, and the now hollow, muscular tube is then boiled and left to dry in the sun. Sun-dried, they can be popped straight into the mouth as a tasty, nutritious snack or stored for up to a year. Once you pop, you can't stop, and people have come up with all sorts of uses for these versatile, desiccated caterpillar carcasses. A favoured approach is to rehydrate and add them to all sorts of dishes, such as *mashonzha* – a spicy stew.

Within their native range, Mopane Worms are a valuable crop and commercially driven overharvesting has seen them disappear from some areas. In other areas though, the long-term sustainability of this important food source comes before commercial interests and only mature caterpillars are harvested.

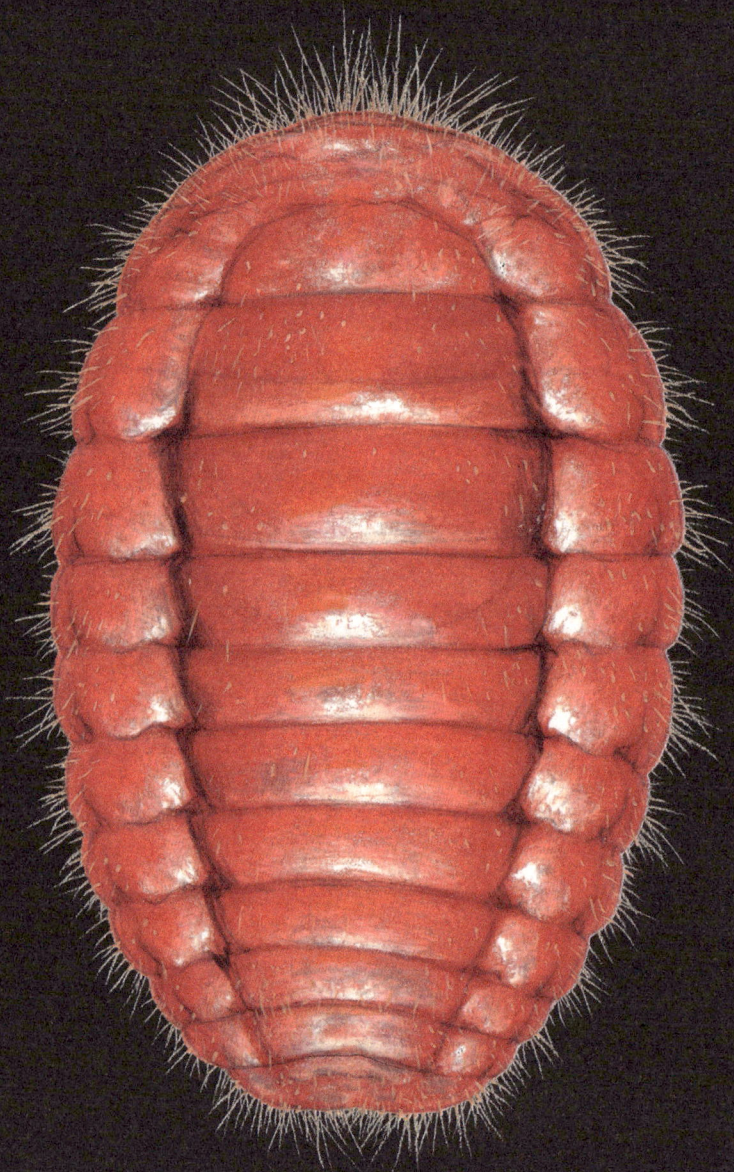

COCHINEAL

These are insects that you've very probably eaten. By that, I don't mean buying a packet of them and popping them into your mouth; rather, their bodies are made into a bright red dye, sometimes called carmine, sometimes called cochineal, which is used as a food colouring in cosmetics and microscopy.

There are several insects that produce this dye, such as the American Cochineal (*Dactylopius coccus*), Armenian Cochineal (*Porphyrophora hamelii* – pictured) and Polish Cochineal (*Porphyrophora polonica*). They all belong to a quirky group of sap-sucking bugs known as scale insects, a group that includes some of the most bizarre insects of all. The females are wingless and immobile, plugged into their host plant via their straw-like mouthparts through which they suck the plant's sap. Soft, plump and sessile, they've evolved various means of defence against their many predators, including waxy coatings in some species and harder coverings that look a bit like a scale in others, hence the common name.

In scale insects we can see just about the entire gamut of animal reproductive strategies. Nothing is off the table for scale insects. You will need to pay close attention to this bit because it can all get rather confusing. Good old, standard sexual reproduction is practised; albeit by females and males that look wildly different. Males are fully winged and often much smaller than their mates. In contrast, the females don't mature outwardly, but look like youngsters their entire life – a phenomenon called neoteny. In some of these sexual species, males might only develop from unfertilized eggs, while females develop from fertilized eggs. Hermaphrodites are very rare in insects, but scale insects are this too: the adults in these species have a combined ovary and testis. Males are an expensive and often irritating extravagance for any species, so some scale insects have dispensed with them altogether – the females simply cloning themselves. There are pros and cons to this. Pros: no males; cons: extinction by inbreeding, eventually.

American Cochineal reproduce sexually, with the small, winged males only living long enough to disperse and find a mate. The females – plump, oval and adorned with a layer of protective greyish wax – live out their entire lives on the foodplant, feeding on its sap. The carminic acid within their body, which is what we process into carmine, is a feeding deterrent that gives them a degree of protection from predators. Still, lots of enemies have sidestepped this defence and greedily feed on them regardless, one of the most interesting of which is the caterpillar of a type of snout moth. Not only do these caterpillars gorge themselves on cochineal eggs and young, but they also salvage the carminic acid from their prey and use it as a defence against their own predators.

Harvesting American Cochineal that survive these depredations is a labour-intensive process, and one that goes back at least 2,000 years.

BEE ROBBER FLY

n English, flies within the family Asilidae are variously known as Robber Flies or Assassin Flies – a nod to their fiercely predatory lifestyle. Both adults and larvae are active hunters equipped with a venomous bite. Cosmopolitan in distribution, this is a very diverse bunch of flies, with more than 7,400 species currently known and many more still to be described. The large size of some species as well as their behaviour – darting from perches to hunt other insects, catching their prey in mid-air – makes them rather conspicuous. I've watched a 4-cm-long species in southern Peru, perched on a twig in a sunny glade, its head twitching this way and that, scanning the air for prey.

As its name suggests, the Bee Robber Fly pretends to be a bee, a disguise that offers some protection from its own predators, namely birds, who associate this general appearance with stings and pain. In the places you find these flies, you'll see them perched on logs waiting for prey to fly past, zooming off to intercept the prey and dispatch it with a venomous bite.

These formidable, active hunters depend on vision, but as they are small there's simply not room for a huge number of photoreceptors – light-gathering cells, which are roughly the same size regardless of the animal. One way these flies get around this limitation is with larger lenses right in the centre of each compound eye. The photoreceptors are set further back from these lenses than in the rest of the eye, which provides a high resolution zone in the centre of the insect's field of view. This is similar to the fovea in your eye, which is a small region of the retina that provides the sharpest vision.

Another ingenious trick these flies possess to accurately track and chase hinges on their ability to see the specific wing-beat frequency of their preferred prey. As the prey flies past, its wings will catch the light, the frequency of these flashes piquing the interest of the Robber Fly. Using twitchy, super-fast movements of its head called saccades, the fly tracks these flashes, its brain predicting the path of the prey and allowing it to dart from its perch and intercept its quarry in mid-air.

Obviously, there's quite a bit of interest in the visual systems and flight control of these aerial hunters. Combining visual systems with artificial intelligence technology could, for example, underpin significant advances in autonomous vehicles.

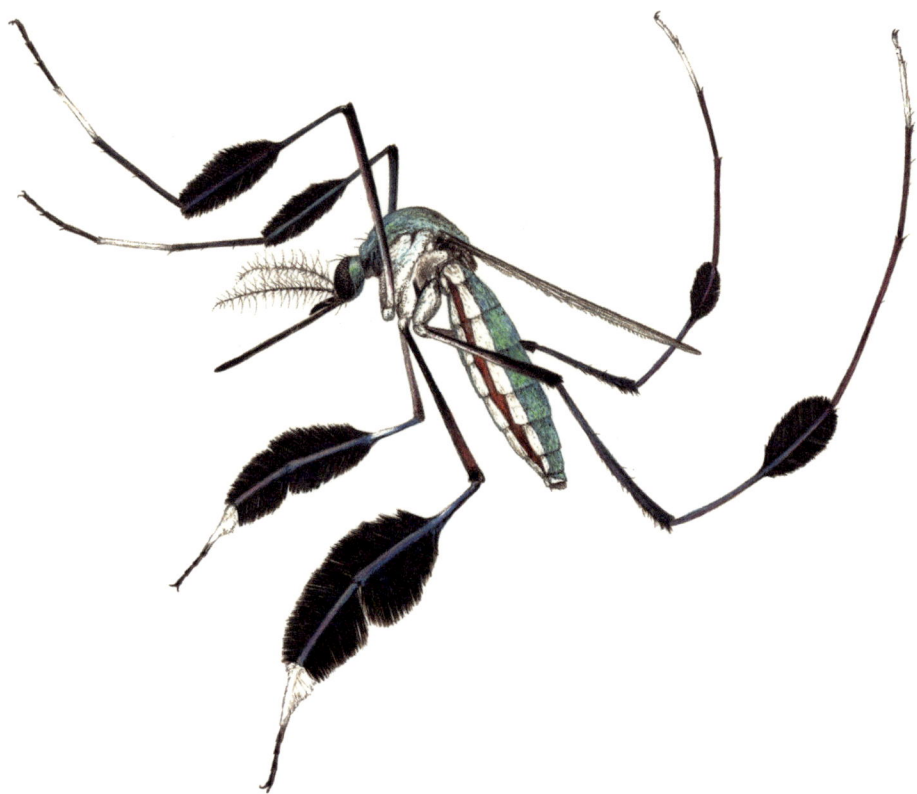

SABETHES MOSQUITO

I speak to you now on behalf of the Mosquito Appreciation Society. I realize this is a very hard sell, given the proclivity of some of these animals for sucking our blood and transmitting a panoply of diseases, causing more than a million deaths every year.

All this disease and death has spurred a huge amount of research – enough to fill a good-sized library. In seeking to eradicate and control mosquitoes, every aspect of their biology has been forensically scrutinized, making them among the most well known of all the animals. Ecologically, they're extremely successful. The aquatic larvae strain edible morsels from the water with their bristly mouthparts, while the adults deftly suck plant and animal juices – a way of life that goes back at least 125 million years. In some species, the females suck blood in order to mature their eggs, which is the real rub because parasitic organisms exploit them as an efficient means of getting from one host to another.

Even here, among these most maligned of insects, we can find remarkable beauty. Look no further than *Sabethes*. These delicate mosquitoes, with their iridescent scales and elegant leg fringes, are found in Central and South America. The females flick their eggs into the small pools of water that accumulate in epiphytic plants (i.e. plants that grow on other plants but are not parasitic), bamboo internodes, fallen banana leaves and hollow seed pods. Here, the larvae glean bacteria and algae from the water using their bristly mouthparts, sometimes also attacking and killing other mosquito larvae competing for food in the same pool. Eventually, the larvae pupate and turn into winged adults.

Life is short for the adults, so they waste no time in trying to find a mate. Perched on the underside of a branch or twig, a receptive female, waiting to be wooed, releases pheromones that quickly attract a male. In his opening gambit, a hopeful male flies in tight loops, holding his feathery legs outstretched to show them off. He then alights on the perch, face to face with the female, and embraces her tenderly with one of his feathery legs, while he waves his other free legs in an arc. If this display is to the female's pleasing – if she likes his colours and moves – she lowers her abdomen to allow copulation. If it's not, she kicks him off and waits for another male.

Once mated, the females must secure a blood meal to mature the eggs in their abdomens. They do sometimes suck blood from humans, especially from noses, but other animals, perhaps birds or monkeys, are the preferred hosts. The way in which they feed is as remarkable as the rest of their biology. Using their flexible, straw-like mouthparts, they navigate the tough, outer layers of the skin, locating a capillary to pierce and drink from. They also inject saliva, which is a cocktail of different compounds, some of which prevent the blood from clotting, while others modulate the host's immune response.

THISTLEDOWN VELVET ANT

I f ever there was an insect worthy of being called a punk, it is this Thistledown Velvet Ant (*Dasymutilla gloriosa*). A type of Velvet 'ant', this is a family of around 7,000 species of wasp, the females being wingless and resembling large, furry ants, hence the common name. The winged males look very different to the females, so much so that you could mistake them for different species.

Native to the arid regions of the American Southwest and down into Mexico, the females of this particular species of Velvet Ant sport a pelt of bright white hairs that, to our eyes at least, give them more than a passing resemblance to the fruits of the creosote bush. Given the resemblance, it was long assumed that this must be camouflage – the Velvet Ant afforded some protection from its predators by looking like the fuzzy fruits.

The thing is, human eyes see the world in a certain way, so what we assume to be mimicry is not always the case. Eager to discover if this fuzzy insect was actually mimicking the creosote bush fruits, biologists did some sleuthing. It turns out the creosote bush is a relative newcomer to Mexico and the American Southwest, colonizing these lands from South America at some point during the last ice age, about 100,000 years ago. In contrast, this Velvet Ant has been scuttling around those arid lands for about five million years, so the resemblance to the fruits must be a coincidence. The biologists found that the spectrum of light reflected by the Velvet Ant's bright white hairs was rather different to that reflected by the fruits of the creosote bush. For one thing, the Velvet Ant reflects much more UV light than the fruit; therefore, it probably looks very different to a bird or a lizard – the main predators of these insects.

What, then, is the purpose of this bright white fluff? More questions and measurements provided some intriguing insights. It seems the reflective hairs of the Velvet Ant are more about staying cool, reflecting the sun's heat and preventing it from being cooked as it trundles around on the baked ground.

Velvet Ants are nest parasites, typically of ground-nesting bees and wasps. Frantically active, the females search out the nests of their hosts, slip inside and deposit an egg in each brood chamber. The Velvet Ant larva hatches and consumes the young of the nest maker and the provisions within the brood chamber. The heat-reflecting fuzz gives this species an edge in that it can remain active and seek out host nests in the heat of the day when its predators are forced to take shelter.

DASYMUTILLA GLORIOSA ├──────────────────

SAHARAN SILVER ANT

The deserts of North Africa are some of the most extreme environments on Earth. Surface temperatures in the midday sun can reach a staggering 70°C, which is more than enough to effectively cook any living thing. Well, almost any, as, in the words of Michael Crichton by way of Dr Ian Malcolm: 'life finds a way.' Enter the Saharan Silver Ant (*Cataglyphis bombycina*) – a dashing insect, both literally and figuratively, that has found a way to survive and thrive in this oven.

These ants are active hunters, leaving the relative safety of their subterranean nests to forage on the baking surface in the heat of the day when most other living things are holed up, waiting for life to cool down. Their prey are other insects and invertebrates that have made the mistake of venturing out in the day's heat and which have succumbed to it.

In preparation for these foraging missions into the desert oven, these ants have a neat metabolic trick. All living things produce special proteins called 'heat-shock proteins' to protect their delicate cellular workings from high temperatures. In most animals, these are produced in the response to heat, but the ants have evolved an ability to synthesize the proteins before they go out to forage, while they're still in the relative cool of the nest. Doing this prepares the ant's body in advance for the high temperatures it will encounter.

These heat-shock proteins allow the ants to tolerate much higher temperatures than most other animals, but they do have a limit – a critical thermal maximum of

53.6°C. If their internal temperature exceeds this limit they're toast, which means they have only a few minutes to find food and get it back to the safety of the nest. Fortunately, they're extremely fleet of foot and one of the fastest animals on the planet, for their size. They scamper along at 3.1 km/h. Granted, this doesn't sound like much, but it would be like you or I tearing around at 720 km/h, which is nearly 20 times faster than an Olympic gold medallist.

[They are] one of the fastest animals on the planet, for their size.

Although stylish, the silvery hairs covering the body of this ant also have a vital function – namely reflecting light and heat. Viewed through an electron microscope, these hairs have a triangular cross section, a shape that allows them to reflect the sun's rays as well offloading heat from the ant's body. This silvery, hairy coating reduces the temperature of the ant by 5 to 10°C, inspiring biomimetic engineers to fabricate flexible structures that are also able to both dissipate and reflect radiative heat.

As if the super heat-shock proteins, extreme speed and reflective coating were not enough, the ants also have supreme powers of navigation. Not only do they count their steps, but they also do frequent pirouettes to orientate to the position of the sun and memorized landmarks. This in-built GPS allows them to make the most of the time they have in the open and to find their way back to the nest without getting lost, which would be fatal.

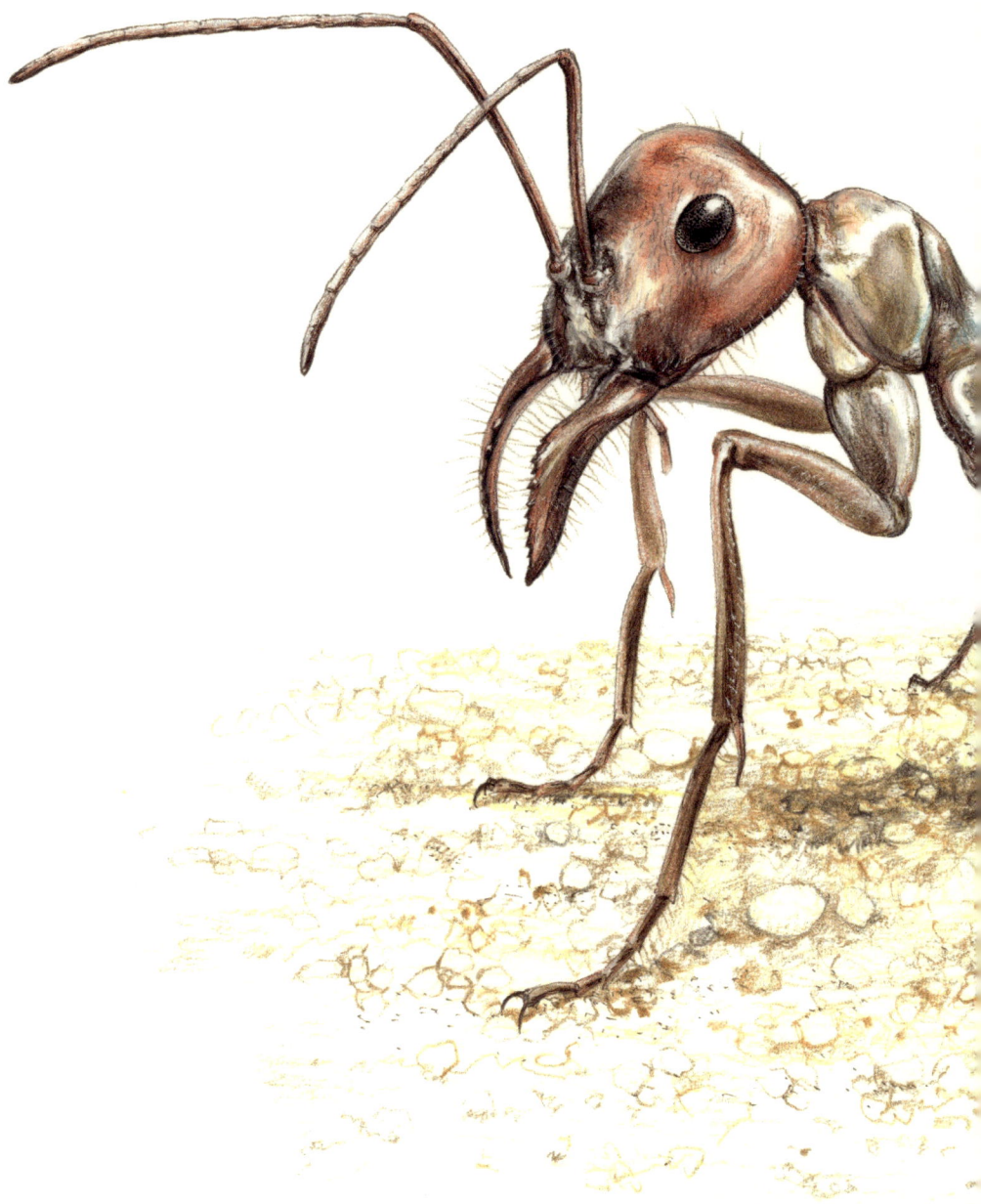

Reflective hairs and a suite of other adaptations allow this ant to forage for short periods in the blistering heat of the Sahara.

RAJAH BROOKE'S BIRDWING

The Rajah Brooke's Birdwing (*Trogonoptera brookiana*) is a stonking creature, one of the largest butterflies, and something of a conservation icon. The microscopic structure of the wing scales combined with pigments creates a visual feast of neon green and red flashes on a velvety black background. The males in particular are nothing if not conspicuous. I've seen large numbers of the males 'puddling' at the edge of a river in Borneo, sucking up moisture and salts through their long proboscis. The females are less conspicuous, as they're more concerned with finding Dutchman's pipe, a toxin-laden vine on which their caterpillars feed. As they feed, the caterpillars assimilate these toxins into their tissues, which are retained into adulthood and advertised by the bright markings of the adult butterfly – a warning to predators.

The name of this butterfly is a tribute to James Brooke, a privileged soldier who was born in India. He lived during what was the peak of the British Empire, a time of incredible achievements, but also very questionable, domineering policies. In 1841, the Sultan of Brunei offered Brooke the governorship of Sarawak for his help in quelling the rampant piracy in the region. Brooke wanted more, though, and in 1842, he became the Rajah of Sarawak. Extraordinary times. Brooke helped grease the wheels of Wallace's expedition through the Malay Archipelago (see page 80), for which many species were named in his honour.

Found through a swathe of the steamy forests of Southeast Asia, from Sumatra, through the Riau Archipelago and Peninsular Malaysia to Borneo, the national butterfly of Malaysia has graced stamps, artwork and tourism bumf thanks to its appearance and plight. These forests – ancient, beautiful places teeming with life – have been destroyed at a terrifying rate to make way for monocrops such as palm oil. I've been to some of these forests and no description can do them justice. They include towering trees and a panoply of superb animals: parachuting frogs and geckos, gliding snakes, gibbons and orangutans to name just a few.

As well as habitat loss, this butterfly is also threatened by collectors who seek specimens for the butterfly trade. This threat has resulted in official protection for the Rajah Brooke's Birdwing. It is illegal for any specimens of this butterfly to be exported without a permit, but this doesn't stop serious smugglers even though the penalties for getting caught are not to be sniffed at. Wildlife traffickers can illicitly move all sorts of animals across borders, so insect specimens are not much of a challenge.

HOODED KATYDID

Katydids, also known as Bush Crickets, represent a large group of insects, comprising more than 8,000 species, the vast majority of which are found in the tropics. They resemble grasshoppers, but are distinguished by their long, thin antennae. Many of them are masters of camouflage, mimicking living and dead leaves, even lichen. In some species, the subtlety of this mimicry has to be seen to be believed, right down to fake leaf veins, fungal spots, herbivore damage and their ability to stay statue still for long periods in postures that enhance the disguise.

The impressive camouflage of these insects has been driven by the fact that so many things want to eat them because they're a substantial parcel of protein, fats and other nutrients. Many of them are very large – this particular species from New Guinea and Australia, *Siliquofera grandis*, is up to 13 cm long with a wingspan up to 27 cm. Their size means they're on the menu for birds, mammals, reptiles, other insects and spiders. In Costa Rica, I've seen troupes of capuchin monkeys scouring the low canopy of coastal forest for insects, particularly resting Katydids. Sometimes the Katydids narrowly escape, losing an appendage or two to the marauding monkeys, but other times the monkeys are too fast, grabbing the Katydids with their quick hands to greedily devour them.

It is during the night when Katydids are active, but even then, when most of their enemies are asleep, they're still not safe. Perhaps their greatest, nocturnal nemeses are bats that listen in to the Katydid's courtship songs, normally produced by rubbing the wings together. One wing functions as a scraper, while the other has a file of tiny teeth, producing a song that is unique to each species. The name 'Katydid' comes from the three-pulsed call – ka-ty-did – of one particular species. A tropical forest at night is filled with a cacophony of these songs, as well as other sounds that form a nocturnal soundscape, much of which is beyond the range of human hearing. These songs allow the males to impress the females, as well as enabling them to find each other in the tangle of trees, bushes and vines where they live. Bats eavesdrop on these songs, pinpointing the location of the performers and swooping out of the darkness to grab them. The Katydids do have a trick up their sleeve, though, because their ears, on their front legs, are as sensitive as the bats' hearing. They can hear the distinctive echolocation pulses of an approaching bat and know to then fall silent, avoiding detection of their exact location.

SILIQUOFERA GRANDIS ├────────────────────────────────┤ NEW GUINEA

MAMMOTH WASP

Along with Tarantula Hawk Moths (see page 60), Mammoth Wasps are the largest wasps on the planet, and certainly the chunkiest. Their common name is in reference to their heft and in life they are quite a sight. In the North African spring, I've seen huge numbers of female Mammoth Wasps, scudding around meadows on their glittering wings looking for nectar and their hosts. The iridescence of the wings perhaps gives them some protection from predators, drawing attention to their bright, aposematic colours. These colours broadcast that the females have a sting and that they know how to use it.

This particular Mammoth Wasp (*Megascolia procer*) is found across a swathe of Asia from India through to Java. Like other Mammoth Wasps, the female has thick powerful legs, an adaptation for burrowing, which is a strange way of life for an adult wasp. It needs to burrow to find the fat beetle grubs on which its larvae will develop. Such hosts can be found in the soil and in the powdery detritus that accumulates within hollow trees and stumps. The hosts of this species are the plump grubs of the magnificent, tri-horned Atlas Beetle and its relatives.

In a complex habitat, the search for these hosts is guided by odours – the female wasp detecting minute quantities of chemicals in the air which betray the presence of the hidden, subterranean beetle grubs. Following a trail of these odours to their source, first on the wing and then on foot, the female tunnels down into the substrate, eventually locating her prize.

The wasp grabs the beetle larva with her curved mandibles, shifting it around to get it in the correct position to bring her sting to bear. She stings the larva on the underside of each of its segments apart from the last three. The female wasp doesn't bother with these last three segments because they lack ganglia – small bundles of nerve fibres that act like a mini brain for each segment. The venom injected by the sting causes paralysis. As an aside, I have first-hand experience of their venom after being stung by a Mammoth Wasp in Peru. The venom actually did very little, which is not surprising given I wasn't the prospective host.

Once the beetle larva is sufficiently paralysed, the female wasp lays an egg on it and departs to seek out more hosts. After a few days, the wasp larva hatches, consumes everything but the exoskeleton of the host and then constructs a cocoon underground in which it pupates. When they emerge, adult Mammoth Wasps are very fond of nectar and might be quite useful pollinators. The males of some species are even duped into being the specialist pollinators of certain orchid species, the flower mimicking the odour and appearance of the female wasp. In attempting to mate with the flower, the male wasp picks up a sticky mass of pollen that it then carries to other flowers.

EMERALD COCKROACH WASP

n many species of venomous animal, the substances injected via a sting or a bite have evolved into much more than just a means of killing prey and hurting predators. In some parasitoid wasps, the venom has become so sophisticated that it controls the behaviour of the prey, affecting its movement and activity.

The Emerald Cockroach Wasp (*Ampulex compressa*) is one such insect. This flying jewel preys exclusively on cockroaches. Using its powerful senses, it homes in on an unwary cockroach, tussles with it and curves its flexible abdomen around to deliver the first of two stings. This first sting is directed into the tiny nodes of the central nervous system located in the cockroach's thorax, which control its legs. The venom blocks the activity of these nerve cells, causing a transient paralysis that lasts for about two to five minutes.

With its prey temporarily incapacitated, the wasp must work quickly and deftly to deliver its second sting. With surgical precision, guided by sensory structures on the tip of its sting, the wasp delivers a tiny dose of venom to a region of the cockroach's brain, which controls, among other things, its escape reflex.

The cockroach quickly recovers from the temporary paralysis of the first sting, but the second sting has rendered it a zombie. Rather than making a sharp exit for the nearest bit of cover, the cockroach simply stays put, fixatedly grooming itself for around 30 minutes, while the wasp scoots off to look for a suitable lair.

On its return, the wasp gives the cockroach a hint of what's in store by biting off one of its antennae and lapping at the blood which flows from the severed appendage. Rather than just a welcome snack, this might also allow the wasp to check the dosing of its venom. The wasp then leads the cockroach to the refuge it found earlier, leading it by an antenna like a docile pet. There, the wasp lays a single egg on the zombified host.

The cockroach, stupefied but still alive and able to groom itself, is sealed in this hideaway with small stones and other debris, not to prevent it from escaping – it has no urge to – but to keep it safe from predators. The wasp larva hatches to find itself sitting on a mound of self-cleaning food, which it starts tucking into. After two days, the young larva is big enough to tunnel into the host and, after four or five days, the wasp larva has nearly entirely consumed the cockroach. After about eight days, the wasp larva is ready to pupate, and it spins itself a silken cocoon inside the drying casket of the cockroach. The adult hatches after about four weeks to begin the cycle again.

As macabre as this might seem, this lifestyle is extremely important ecologically because insects like this wasp are crucial in regulating the population of other insects and spiders. In the places where this wasp occurs, it is a welcome guest in houses because it helps to control pest cockroaches. It was even introduced into Hawaii to control pest cockroaches there – alas, without much success.

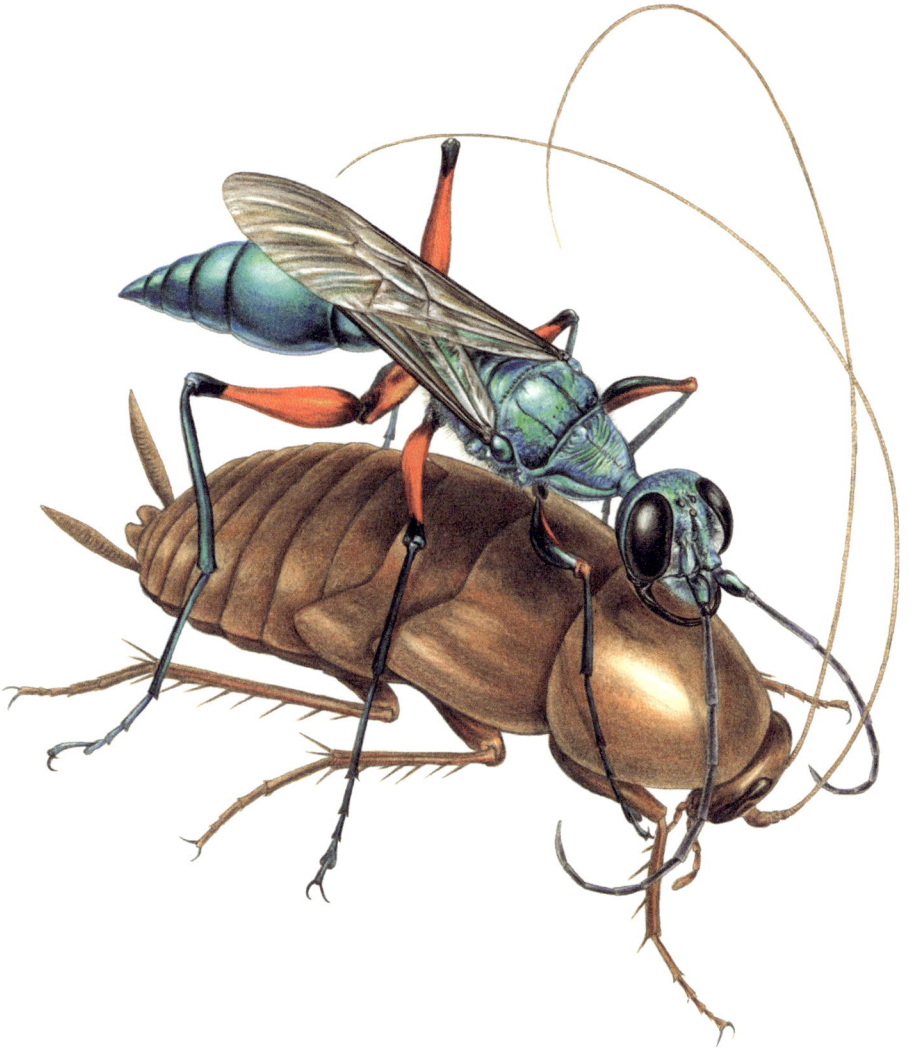

AMPULEX COMPRESSA ├─────────────┤ TROPICAL AFRICA AND ASIA

HEADLIGHT BEETLE

n the gathering darkness of a Costa Rican forest, I was met by an astonishing sight – lots of tiny green 'headlights' careering through the gloom accompanied by the unmistakable buzz of insect wings. The extraordinary lights belong to the Headlight Beetle, a type of large Click Beetle. The green light of the Headlight Beetle is remarkably bright – bright enough to read by and perhaps the brightest light of any insect. In flight, an orange light on their abdomen, reminiscent of a tail light, is also visible.

The production of light by a living thing is exquisite and beetles are masters at it. In the light-producing organs of insects, an enzyme, luciferase, gets to work on its substrate, luciferin, yielding light as a by-product from the chemical reaction. Unlike a filament light bulb which gets ferociously hot, the chemical reaction in the insect is extremely efficient, producing barely any heat. Modern LED lights are very efficient and produce very little heat, but they're still not as efficient as nature's lights.

The beetles are not using their lights to find their way; rather, they are using them to broadcast their toxicity to potential predators, a signal that is copied by a group of perfectly palatable, light-bearing cockroaches. Headlight Beetle larvae are also equipped with lights. Many of these are denizens of dead and decaying wood, but a species from the Cerrado in Brazil lives in burrows in abandoned termite mounds. At night, these mounds can be a constellation of green lights – hundreds, even thousands of beetle larvae, all of whom are trying to attract their dinner. Enticed by the greenish glow, other insects, such as winged termites, alight on the mounds and are promptly snaffled by the beetle larvae.

The green light of the Headlight Beetle is bright enough to read by …

The family of beetles to which the Headlight Beetles belong – the Click Beetles – is a diverse bunch of around 10,000 species with a characteristic elegant shape. When threatened by a predator, a Click Beetle drops to the ground and plays dead, lying on its back. When the hungry mammal or bird approaches to investigate, the beetle employs its secret defence and jolts into the air with an audible click. It might do this repeatedly until the predator has been startled off. This ingenious defence is all down to a catch-like mechanism on the underside of the beetle's thorax. Using muscles and the supremely elastic protein resilin, the thorax articulates to open the catch. When the time is right, the catch springs explosively back to its closed position, flinging the beetle into the air with a click.

HEADLIGHT BEETLE

The twin lights of this beetle produce a brilliant, green glow – the brightest light produced by any insect.

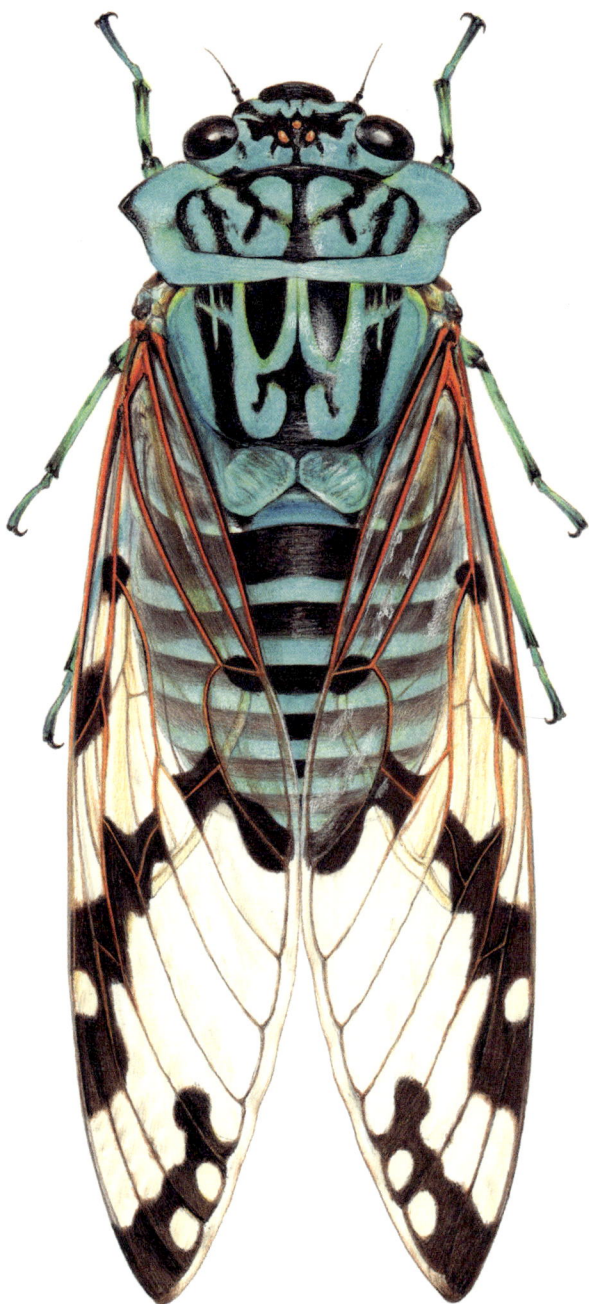

ZAMMARA SMARAGDINA ├─────────────┤ CENTRAL & SOUTH AMERICA

CICADA

These bright, blue-green cicadas (*Zammara smaragdina*) are found in the tropical forests of Central and South America. In lots of places around the world, cicadas make an almighty racket. Weird, wonderful and sometimes downright irritating, cicada song is the natural daytime soundtrack of the places where they abound. Worldwide, more than 3,000 species of cicada are known and all of them have their own unique song. Depending on the species, these range from calls that are beyond the range of our hearing up to what sound like ear-splitting alarms, loud enough to make you jump when they start up nearby. The loudest of these can be 120 decibels, among the loudest sounds produced by any animal.

It is the male cicadas that produce these songs, using a pair of membranous, ribbed structures on their abdomen known as tymbals. Attached to muscles that contract and relax, the tymbals buckle and spring back extremely quickly, the vibrations moving through the air in the largely hollow abdomen, which is a bit like a boom box, amplifying the sound, which is directed through the animal's large eardrums on the underside of its abdomen. These eardrums crumple when the animal is calling, to protect its own ears from the din.

Cicadas are sap-sucking true bugs with a twist: as youngsters they feed underground, using strong, modified front legs to burrow down as much as 2.5 m and to excavate chambers around the tree roots from which they suck sap. The time spent underground varies from as little as two years in some species to 17 years in others. The well-known periodical cicadas of North America emerge en masse as adults every 13 or 17 years. Exactly why is unclear, but it may be to give them a chance against their many predators. When the adults of some species are getting ready to emerge, they construct hollow towers of mud that sprout from the forest floor, almost overnight.

The sap that cicadas guzzle through their straw-like mouthparts is basically sugary water, containing precious little of the other nutrients the cicada needs, especially the female who must mature her eggs. To glean enough nutrients from this liquid, they must imbibe prodigious quantities of it, as much as 300 times their own bodyweight per day. Residing in their gut are a number of symbiotic micro-organisms that get to work on the sap, digesting it and producing the amino acids and other key nutrients the cicada needs. Without these microbes, surviving on sap would be impossible. All the excess water needs to be eliminated quickly as pee, squirted out in high-speed jets, spraying vegetation and the ground. Some desert cicadas even use this excess water to help them keep cool, extruding it from special pores from where it spreads and evaporates.

WARTY LEAF BEETLE

This lumpy character is a type of leaf beetle. One of the largest families of beetles with about 37,000 known species, these beetles clung on to the coat tails of plant evolution which bloomed and diversified into a dizzying array of new forms about 100 million years ago during the heyday of the dinosaurs. As new types of plants evolved, these herbivorous beetles adapted to the new opportunities and surged in diversity. Many leaf beetles, as their name suggests, like to hang out on the leaves of their host plants. This, coupled with their often bright colours and patterns as well as their liking for our crops and ornamental plants, makes them among the more well-known beetles. I'm sure you've heard of the Colorado Potato Beetle, the Lily Beetle and the Rosemary Beetle. These are all types of leaf beetle.

Warty Leaf Beetles are special though. Unlike other leaf beetles, where the larvae feed in or on the same foodplant as the adults, these barrel-shaped beauties have evolved a more left-field approach. This species and its relatives are known as case-bearing leaf beetles, or, more simply, pot beetles.

When the female pot beetle lays an egg, she expertly holds it in a cup-like depression at her rear end, rotating it deftly with her back feet and coating it with small, flattened plates of her own faeces, eventually completely encasing it, forming what looks like a titchy pinecone. As a student, I spent a lot of time watching these beetles. I would watch, enthralled, as the female went through this routine, taking about 15 or 20 minutes to carefully cover each of her eggs.

Once finished, the female casually flicks the egg case off into the leaf litter or attaches it to the plant she's sitting on. When the beetle larva hatches, it breaks out of the case a little bit, enough to get its tough head and strong legs out. It then scuttles off, the case held aloft. At any sign of danger, the tiny larva retreats into the case, its hard, angular head acting like a stopper. Feeding on leaf litter or fresh plant material, the larva must expand its excrement case in order to grow. To do this, it nibbles a lengthways slit in the case, widens it and fills the gap with a paste fashioned from its own droppings mixed with saliva. When the time is right, the larva seals up the case, turns around and pupates. The adult nibbles a perfect cap in the end of the case, pops it open and escapes.

The adults are active insects, scuttling around on their foodplants and taking to the wing readily. When danger looms, they reflexively fold in their legs and antennae and tumble to the ground. In the Warty Leaf Beetles, this behaviour is enhanced by their appearance. Lying on the ground, motionless, they look remarkably like caterpillar droppings.

SIZE

GIANT DOBSONFLY

The purpose of this book is to give you a flavour of the extraordinary diversity of insects, encouraging you to marvel at them the same way I do. However, there were always going to be a couple that might elicit the jitters. The Giant Dobsonfly (*Protohermes grandis*) is one such species; an embodiment of all the things that make some people want to reach for the rolled-up newspaper, although in this case, a cricket bat might be more appropriate.

Granted, this is one medieval-looking insect, its front end alone redolent of some mythical horned beast from a bestiary, but as with the vast majority of insects, it is harmless … mostly. I say 'mostly' because the female Dobsonfly has short, powerful mandibles that can deliver quite a nip – as do the larvae (also known, delightfully, as hellgrammites). The males, as always, are all about their ornaments, specifically the long, sickle-shaped mandibles. These are too long and unwieldy to be of any use for biting would-be enemies; rather, they're put to use in ritualized courtship battles between males. Like rutting stags or testosterone-addled mountain goats, two male Dobsonflies face each other and lock mandibles, the contest played out on a riverine rock or log until one of the combatants gets flipped or displaced from the arena. An opportunity to mate with any females in attendance is the prize.

After the excitement of watching the wrestling and mating with the victor, the female retires to the water's edge, depositing her eggs between the stones there. The larvae, when they eventually hatch, are fully aquatic animals equipped with gills, and they live out their entire existence partially concealed among the stones on the stream bed, snatching any animal smaller than themselves with their powerful mandibles. It might be several years before they have grown sufficiently to pupate, at which point they take their leave of the water to seek out a spot, the soil beneath a rock or log perhaps, where they will metamorphose. In some places, thunderstorms can trigger a mass exodus of mature hellgrammites, as they leave the water to pupate.

As is the way for so many other insects, the adults, when they emerge, have fleetingly short lives. In some of the better-known species, the males live a mere three days, just enough time to have a scrap and to mate. The females live a bit longer, but still only manage about 10 days. The Giant Dobsonfly, when it finally emerges as an adult, is something of a behemoth, with a wingspan approaching 22 cm, the largest of any aquatic insect. Found throughout southern China and into northern Vietnam, the Giant Dobsonfly is acutely sensitive to water and light pollution. Water pollution harms and kills the larvae, while artificial lighting is extremely attractive to the adults, who waste precious moments of their ephemeral lives fluttering futilely around the nearest streetlamp.

PROTOHERMES GRANDIS ├──────────────   ──────────────┤ VIETNAM & CHINA

TARANTULA HAWK WASP

I was exploring the Brazilian Amazon near a place called Novo Airão with some friends, when what I assumed to be a small bird flew across the path in front of us. A few steps further on, the same thing happened again, but this time I had a better view of the animal. It was a wasp, more specifically, a humongous Tarantula Hawk Wasp. It crossed the path in front of us again, but this time I was prepared, net at the ready. With a swift forehand swipe, I had it in the net. Eager to photograph the wasp, but aware of its very painful sting – the second most painful sting of any insect if the Schmidt Sting Pain Index is to be believed – I was grateful when one of my friends donated some tobacco smoke to placate the now very irate insect. This worked like a charm. The wasp ambled to the opening of the bag and proceeded to groom itself for a couple of minutes, allowing me to look at it closely.

No amount of museum specimens can ever equal the sight of one of these animals alive in the wild – and the same goes for all the species in this book. In life, the radiance, the sheen and the way they move is mesmerizing. This wasp was a thing of true beauty: shimmering wings overlying a body that was mostly a velvety, iridescent black above and clothed with golden hairs underneath.

The biology of these animals is as compelling as their appearance. They belong to a large group of some 5,000 known species of wasp, all of which are specialist predators of spiders. As their common name suggests, Tarantula Hawks seek out and dispatch the largest spiders of all. Zooming around on powerful wings, they pick up the telltale odours of their quarry, following them to their source and doing the last of the tracking on foot, their wings and antennae twitching continuously.

At the entrance to the spider's burrow, the wasp gingerly creeps inside. The spider, hunkered down in its lair, senses the approach of its nemesis and, for reasons that are still unclear, makes a sharp exit past the wasp and into the open, which is exactly what the wasp wants. Using her antennae, the wasp provokes the spider into a threat display where it rears up, brandishing its impressive fangs. Seizing the moment to strike, the wasp holds the spider's second pair of legs aloft and injects, with surgical precision, a paralysing venom into a nerve ganglion – a mini brain – near the base of the legs. Her quarry incapacitated, the wasp may groom herself before lapping at some of the spider's 'blood' from the wound left by her sting. Not only does she derive some nourishment from this, but it also allows her to taste if a sufficient dose of venom was administered. The spider is then sealed up in its own burrow or a new chamber excavated by the wasp, along with one of her eggs. Her work finished, the wasp flies off to seek out more eight-legged victims, leaving her grub, when it hatches, to consume the paralysed spider.

To us, this existence can seem rather dark, rather ghoulish, but we mustn't anthropomorphize. The wasp's actions are not borne out of malice, but simply the imperative to make more wasps. Indeed, if it wasn't for animals like this, Darwin may never have questioned religious hegemony.

The radiance, the sheen and the way they move is mesmerizing.

TARANTULA
HAWK WASP

These enormous, stunning wasps are specialized predators of Tarantulas, which they subdue with their potent venom.

STENUS ROVE BEETLE

At ground level, navigating the channels and spaces in the upper parts of the soil, scuttling around in the leaf litter, under logs and stones and clambering among the lower parts of plants is a kaleidoscopic variety of tiny animals. At the scale of these creatures, grassy tussocks are towering peaks, pools are oceans and meadows are vast forests.

Here, as with any habitat, there are herbivores, scavengers, fierce predators, parasites and parasitoids. Dramas, mostly untold, play out in these places all the time, but these habitats and their denizens are mostly overlooked.

One such group of animals found in these habitats are *Stenus* Rove Beetles. This is one of the largest genera of animals, with around 2,700 known species and many more to be described. These charismatic, large-eyed beetles are very common in the right habitats, deftly negotiating the terrain on the hunt for prey. Extremely active and proficient predators, they stalk and dispatch other small arthropods, such as mites and springtails.

Their secret weapon for catching such quarry is telescopic mouthparts. One section – the labium – can be shot out extremely rapidly by forcing haemolymph – the insect equivalent of blood – into it. Fully extended, the tip of the labium reaches a few millimetres from the beetle. 'This is nothing,' I hear you scoff, but in the world of the tiny this is at least half the beetle's body length and is the difference between securing a meal or going hungry. The whole process is so rapid that the prey has no time to react. Even if they saw the strike coming, the business end of this telescopic labium is studded with hair-like setae and pores that secrete an adhesive substance. The setae and glue snag the prey and allow it to be yanked back to the beetle's waiting mandibles.

As well as telescopic mouthparts, these beetles also have one of the most impressive defences of any animal. Yes, these micro-hunters are truly blessed in bizarre adaptations. Many *Stenus* species are found in waterside habitats, where they wander about on the ground and in the vegetation, shooting their spiky mouthparts out at unsuspecting prey. Their small size and long legs mean they can also take to the water and scull along as if they were walking – their weight supported by the water's meniscus. This in itself is not all that impressive – there are lots of animals that move around on the surface of water.

What sets *Stenus* Rove Beetles apart, though, is that if a predator looms, they can take to the water and squirt out a mixture of chemicals from the glands at the tip of their abdomen. This chemical cocktail spreads over the surface of the water with such force that the beetle is propelled forward at terrific speed – well, relatively. The velocity the beetle reaches is equivalent to 600–900 km/h in human terms and it does this in a fraction of a second – acceleration that would turn you or me inside out. Needless to say, any small predator will be completely bamboozled by the sudden disappearance of its dinner.

BITING MIDGE

No-see-ums, punkies, knotts, five-Os, moose flies. These are just some of the family friendly common names of Biting Midges (*Ceratopogonidae*). There are plenty more too, but these are basically just strings of expletives, often uttered at volume, which you'll understand full well if you've been in a place where these flies abound. Biting Midges are tiny, so they get into all sorts of places where larger flies can't, and their bites are considerably more annoying than their size would suggest. In plenty of temperate places around the world, it is a cruel irony that the only time of year you can go out and enjoy the fleeting summer sun is also when adult female midges are on the wing and looking for blood, which is the reason why they bite.

Granted, midges can be annoying, but they're also fascinating and important insects, not least of all because some of them – one of which is illustrated – pollinate the flowers of the cocoa tree, ultimately giving us the seeds we make into chocolate. More than a fair swap for being annoying? Perversely, chocolate is such a massive industry that it has driven intensive cultivation of the cacao tree, destroying the very habitats the midges depend on. Willy Wonka never told us this, but preserving these ecologically diverse habitats is the only way of keeping the wheels of chocolate production turning.

Not only do they help to furnish us with chocolate, but some of the Biting Midges are also record holders, able to beat their tiny wings faster than any other animal – a truly extraordinary 1,000 times per second. It all comes down to a special type of muscle and the elasticity of the wings and the thoracic box that houses the flight muscles. The flight muscles in these flies – so-called asynchronous muscles – are unique to insects. Unlike normal muscles that require an electrical signal from the nerves for each and every contraction, asynchronous muscles contract many times with each nerve signal and are activated by being stretched. Vertical flight muscles joining the top and bottom of the thorax contract to bring the wings up, distorting the thorax. This distortion stretches the horizontal muscles joining the front and back of the thorax and makes them contract, pivoting the wing downwards and allowing the springy thorax to go back to its original shape, stretching the vertical muscles again to continue the cycle. Consider this for a few moments. All of this is happening 1,000 times a second in a space that is a fraction of one millimetre across! Needless to say, engineers are trying to replicate this mechanism to some degree to power miniature drones.

In some Biting Midges that feed on the blood of other insects, the promise of gorging on food overrides the need to fly. After alighting on a suitable host, these midges feed so greedily and so deeply that they become extremely bloated and rather tick-like. They resign the use of their wings and legs, gripping onto the host by mouthparts alone until, eventually satiated, they drop to the ground, splurge their eggs and die.

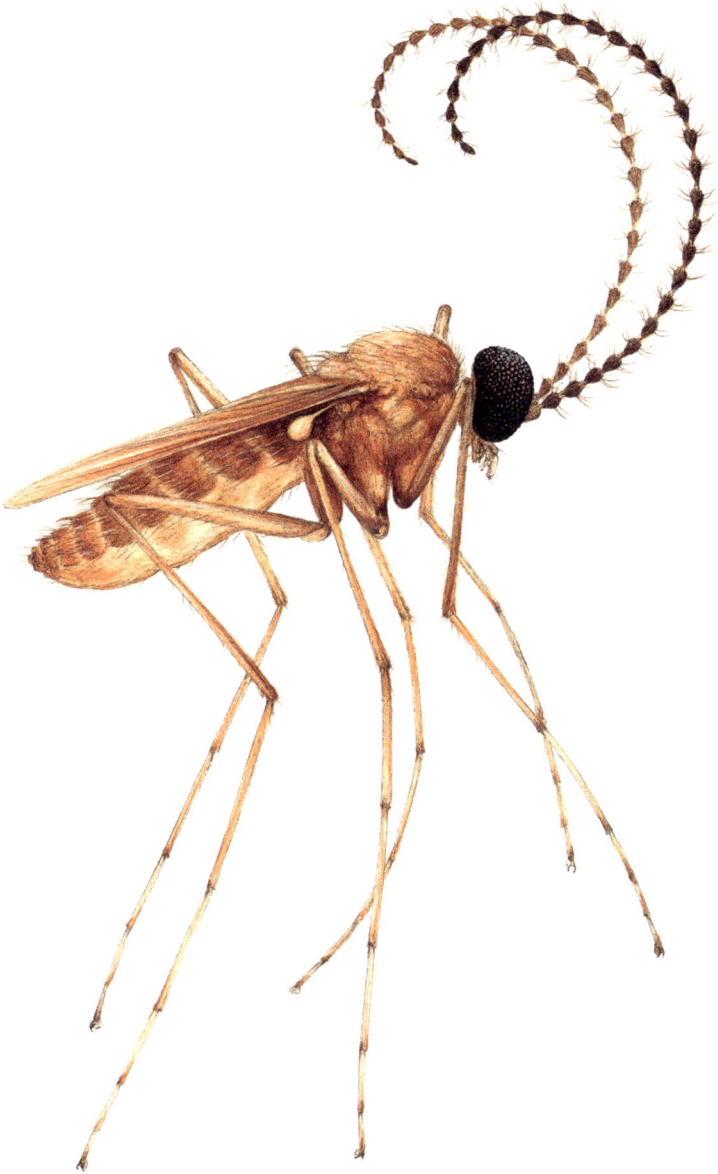

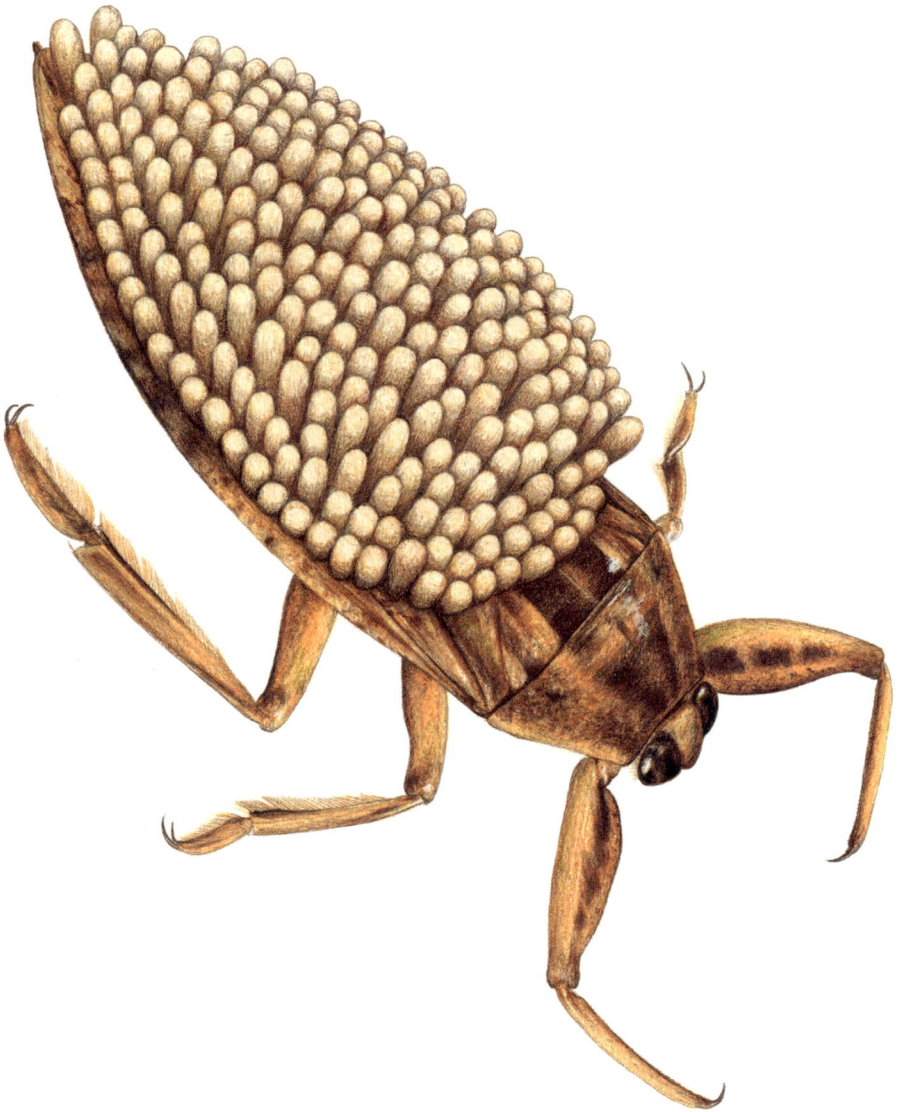

GIANT WATER BUG

There I was, up to my waist in the water of a roadside ditch in the Nariva Swamp, Trinidad. I was looking for insects and helping some friends collect guppies for their research. As well as guppies, a Giant Water Bug was snagged in the seine net we were using and the specimen in front of me was easily 10 cm long. Not only are these bugs big and strong, they also have hooked feet and a venomous bite, said to be excruciatingly painful. This one was also pretty peeved. So, there I was, waist deep in the water, delicately trying to extricate each of the bug's legs from the net, while avoiding the business end – the end with the venomous bite. My hands were wet though, and the bug was gradually turning and trying to bring its stabbing mouthparts to bear. I didn't fancy getting bitten, so I whanged the bug as far as I could. Hastily, I collected a bucket and retrieved it for a better look.

The largest of these aquatic, predatory bugs are more than 12 cm long, making them the largest true bugs by some margin, large enough to catch small fish and amphibians. As an entomologist, I don't use the word 'bug' willy-nilly. I reserve it for the enormous, diverse group of insects that includes aphids, shield bugs, cicadas and the like. Among their defining characteristics are straw-like mouthparts (the rostrum) and a life cycle where there is no metamorphosis. Instead, the young – so-called nymphs – look like miniature adults.

Many true bugs are good parents, with Giant Water Bugs (*Belostomatidae*) being among the most attentive. In most insects that look after the eggs and offspring, it is typically the females that shoulder the burden, with the males flitting around trying to inseminate as many females as possible. In Giant Water Bugs, there's been a role reversal: it is the males that do the parenting, which is very rare in insects. Depending on the species, the male simply guards the eggs, or he carries them on his back, cleaning them with his legs and regularly taking them to the surface so they have enough oxygen. This dedication has a price because the male, weighed down by eggs, finds it harder to hunt and to move about, ultimately reducing his lifespan. This role reversal extends all the way to courtship, too: attentive males with a good bit of dorsal real estate are in demand, and it is the females who must do the wooing.

The paternal care shown by these insects is of little interest to the various people around the world to whom they are something of a delicacy. Although aquatic, the adults of most species are fully winged and are attracted to artificial light while dispersing, which makes them rather easy to catch. They're eaten in parts of the Philippines, Laos, Cambodia and Vietnam, but probably most widely and with the most gusto in Thailand, where they're known locally as *mang da*, which is also used as a slang word for 'pimp' because of the shared propensity for buzzing around streetlights.

LEAFCUTTER ANT

Worker leafcutter ants (*Atta* and *Acromyrmex*) are medium-sized insects, but they dominate ecosystems in a way that bears no relation to the size of the individual ant. These ants form perhaps the most complex insect societies, building enormous and fantastically complex nests that can extend over 600 m2 and plunge eight metres or more into the soil – true wonders of nature. These colossal nests are home to millions of workers, all of which are the offspring of the queen, so fecund she may produce 150 million progeny in her lifetime.

To get an idea of the size and complexity of these nests, you will need the following: a big leafcutter ant nest (obviously); 6.3 tonnes of cement; 8,200 litres of water; and some determined, spade-wielding biologists. Next, find the nest entrances and pour in your cement. Do a spot of birdwatching or insect collecting while the cement hardens and then get digging. Careful excavation will reveal an insect metropolis. Numerous chambers are connected by tunnels, constructed in a way to maximize airflow through the nest and to provide the shortest transport routes – and all of this is the work of animals with brains a little smaller than the next comma. In constructing these nests, the ants have to move tonnes of earth, approximately 40 tonnes for a nest covering only 50 m$_2$. This Herculean task equates to billions of ant-loads of soil, each load carried about 1 km in human terms and weighing four times as much as the ant itself.

The subterranean efforts of the leafcutter ants are matched or even exceeded by what they get up to above ground. In a strange symbiosis – and one of the few examples of farming among animals – leafcutter ants grow and eat a type of fungus, specifically little swellings called gongylidia provided by the fungus. The fungus is cultivated in special gardens held within some of the subterranean chambers. These fungi are found only in the nests of leafcutter ants. The fungus in turn consumes plant matter and this is what the ants have to provide shedloads of, making them the dominant herbivores in the Neotropics. Long lines of foraging workers scuttle off into the surrounding landscape, completely denuding large areas of foliage to keep their fungi fed. In some places, the most abundant types of leafcutter ant account for as much as 17% of all consumed foliage, vastly more than all the large, conspicuous herbivores combined.

The queen [is] so fecund she may produce 150 million progeny in her lifetime.

In the leafcutter-ant colony, there can be several, distinct types of worker. The smallest of these are known as minims and they take care of the brood and tend to the fungus gardens. Next up are the minors, who continuously patrol and defend the foraging lines. It's normal to see a minor worker hitching a ride on a piece of leaf being carried back to the nest, not because they can't be bothered to walk, but because the worker carrying the piece of leaf is at risk from parasitoid flies which develop inside the ants – normally their heads – given half a chance. Like a tiny guard dog, the minor worker keeps these flies at bay. Mediae workers are bigger than the minors and their main job is collecting foliage and returning it to the nest. A few years ago, it was discovered that these mediae workers change tasks when the cutting edge of their zinc-reinforced mandibles – which start out razor-sharp – begin to dull and the task of cutting the leaves takes longer. These older mediae workers then shift to carrying duties. Largest of all the leafcutter workers are the majors. These are the colony's soldiers, but they also do heavy lifting – clearing the foraging trails of larger bits of debris and carrying bulky morsels back to the nest.

The vastly different forms we see in an ant colony are even more remarkable when we consider that they have the same DNA. How do you get adults that look, function and behave so differently from just one set of instructions? In some, if not all, cases, this all depends on what the young insect is fed. Giving lots of food, not enough food or a specific type of food at the appropriate time appears to flick a developmental switch which results in the staggeringly different adult forms.

LEAFCUTTER ANT

The nests of these ants are among the largest, most complex structures made by any animal.

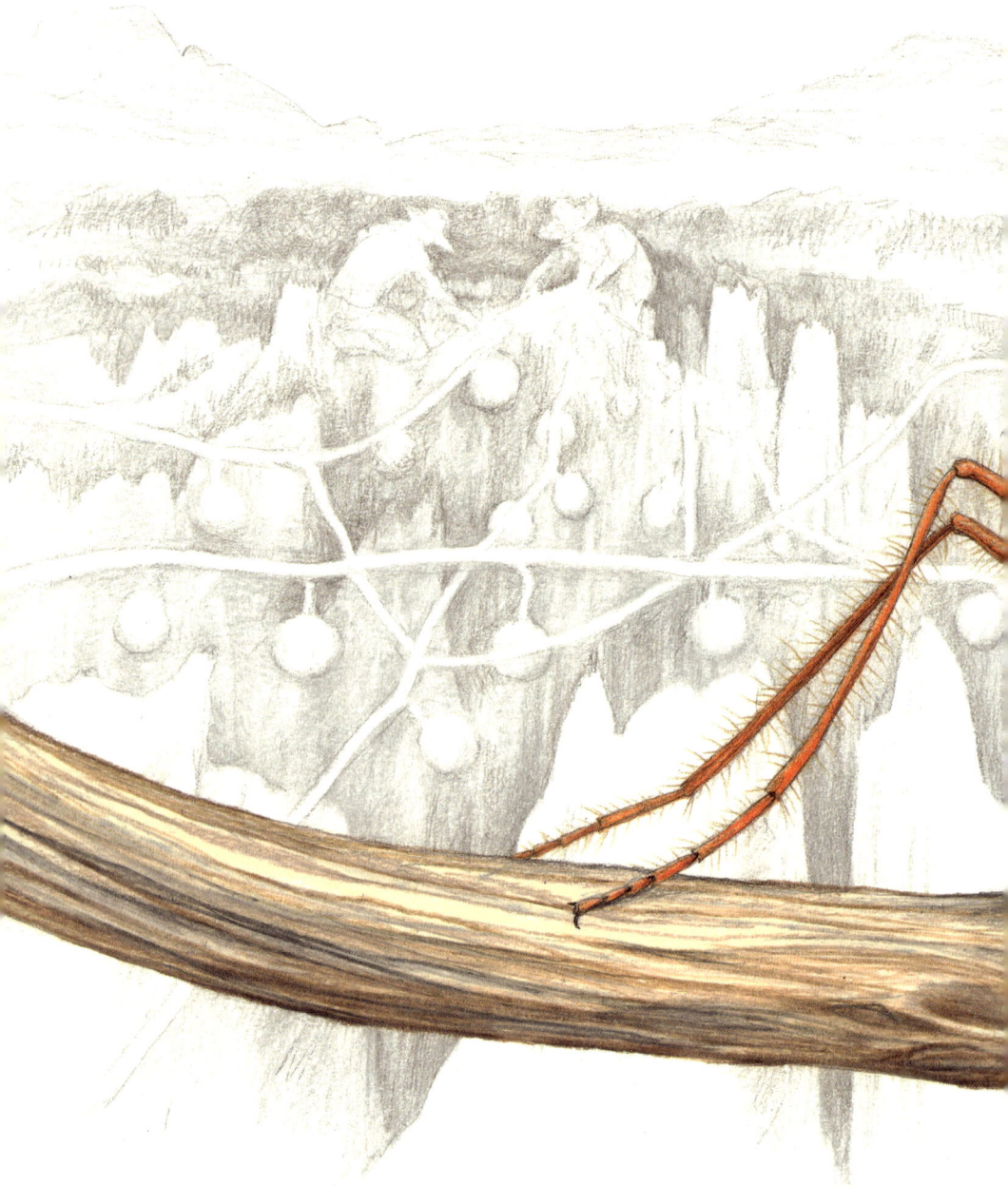

FIG WASP

As familiar as figs are, they are extremely odd. Botanically speaking, the fig is not a fruit; rather, it is a cluster of flowers – an inflorescence – that has turned in on itself to form a roughly spherical structure. This strange form is a result of what is the most intimate and ancient relationship between a plant and an animal – the tiny Fig Wasps (*Agaonidae*) that pollinate the 850 or so species of fig. These tiny wasps are beautifully adapted to life inside these inverted flowers. Ninety million years ago the ancestors of today's Fig Wasps were probably parasites of the trees that would eventually become the fig species we know today, forming galls, or abnormal growths to aid the insects, in the flowers of these trees. The wasps may have done a bit of pollinating on the side, but this was probably incidental. Over time, however, the relationship grew ever more intertwined and today the figs and their wasps are utterly dependent on one another.

Although the end result is pollination, the story that unfolds within each fig to get there as it matures and ripens is one of mutilation, prodigious penises, incest and brutal conflict. It begins with a female Fig Wasp alighting on a fig that is ripe for pollination. She might have flown 10 km, carrying pollen from the fig where she was born, and to enter this new fig, she must take a one-way trip through the fig's ostiole to its centre. This tunnel is so narrow that squeezing through it wrenches her antennae and wings off. Once inside, she sets about laying eggs into the short flowers, pollinating the long flowers until she's exhausted and eventually keels over. Of her brood, it is her sons that emerge first. The males are pallid, wingless, tiny-eyed and yet stout of leg, and the only home they will ever know is the dark, close confines of the fig. In some species, the brothers fight to the death for the right to mate with their sisters who are yet to emerge, using shear-like mouthparts to bite each other's heads off.

Given what you've just read, you won't be surprised to find that Fig Wasp mating is also seriously bizarre; indeed, they put the incest into insect. The male chews a hole in one of the flowers containing one of his fully developed sisters before deploying his enormous, telescopic penis – relatively, one of the largest of any animal – which he pokes in through the hole to copulate with her.

Incest successfully completed, the males then set about chopping down the male flowers within the fig and chewing an escape tunnel for their sisters. Cue the emergence of the females, who purposefully gather pollen from the male flowers, packing it into 'baskets' on their thorax before making for the exit and their one and only flight to a new fig in need of pollination.

You could fill a series of hefty tomes with what has been gleaned about the biology of figs and their wasps.

SABRE-TOOTHED LONGHORN BEETLE

Beetles come in an extraordinary range of shapes and sizes, from the speck-like Featherwing Beetles (see page 96) to monsters like this Sabre-toothed Longhorn Beetle (*Macrodontia cervicornis*) found in the hot, humid forests of South America. While not the heaviest beetle, it is one of the longest and, with its unique patterning, one of the most impressive. The largest individuals of this species approach 18 cm in length, which includes the outsized mandibles of the male. These, as in other male insects with elaborate mandibles, are used in courtship battles between males.

The larva of this beetle, an enormous pallid grub growing up to 21 cm long, is a wood feeder, chewing its way through the timber of dead and moribund softwood trees until it is large enough to pupate. Even with the help of symbiotic microorganisms in its gut which turn this fibrous matter into nutrients the beetle can use, reaching this prodigious size takes an age – up to 10 years.

Beetles have long been held as the most speciose, or diverse, group of insects, although this says more about their collectability rather than their actual diversity. The internet has seen a boom in the trading of insect specimens – just take a look on any of the online auction sites. Institutions and individuals snap these specimens up, regardless of where and how they were captured and exported. Only a tiny number of insect species have any degree of international protection, where it is illegal to harm and collect them in their native habitat. We know so little about the populations of most insects that it is highly likely that many species have been hit hard by collecting for the insect specimen trade.

Private individuals amassing large collections of insects, simply for the reason of having the specimens, are driven by the same urge, one no different to that of stamp collecting. As with any other collectables, the rarest specimens command the highest prices, with some species selling for tens of thousands of dollars. Figures like this are driving impoverished locals and professional collectors into the most biodiverse places on the planet to trap and collect sought-after insect species, many of which are already over-collected and are also up against multiple other challenges, including habitat loss and a changing climate (see page 80 – Wallace's Giant Bee).

Some countries, such as Bhutan, India and Australia, have taken a hard-line approach to stemming the wildlife trade, including insects. In recent years, large fines, deportation, travel bans and even jail sentences have been handed out to European collectors caught with insect loot in these countries. The sad thing is, these laws, although necessary, can make genuine research much more difficult.

MACRODONTIA CERVICORNIS ├────────────┤ TROPICAL SOUTH AMERICA

BEE LOUSE

Compared to our forebears, we don't have many parasites on us these days. Old 'friends' such as body lice, pubic lice and fleas are rather rare today, their lifestyle thwarted by hygiene and our ever-growing desire to be smooth-skinned. Even when our bodies and our hovels were hopping with these unwanted passengers, these ectoparasites were all rather small in comparison to us. Imagine having parasites the size of big edible crabs scuttling over your body. A delightful thought, I'm sure you'll agree, but there are plenty of parasites that are disturbingly large compared to their hosts. Among the most extraordinary of these are the Bee Lice (*Braulidae*), which are not actually lice, but highly modified flies that have forsaken the ability to fly in exchange for clinging tenaciously to honeybees for their entire adult life.

These unusual flies, for want of a better word, look rather cute. Completely wingless and flattened, they look dumpy from above, with pleasing proportions and large, strong legs. Via gradual adaptation to a parasitic way of life, their extraneous senses are on the way to becoming vestigial, with much reduced eyes and antennae that are folded back into grooves. They clamber around nimbly on the body of the host, preferring the head and thorax, making regular forays to the mouthparts of the host to get some food. They either do this by scrambling for the sweet fluids the honeybees regurgitate and share with each other, or they stroke and tickle the upper 'lip' of the bee until it extends its tongue, regurgitating a small amount of nectar.

Although they can be found on any bee in the colony, Bee Lice have a definite preference for the queen, since she is long-lived, spends nearly all of her life in the nest and is lavished with attention from her daughters, which includes lots of food. In a nest with a heavy burden of these parasitic flies, the queen may have as many as 100 of them clambering all over her, robbing her food and generally making things difficult. In every other respect, the queen is well defended, so why don't the workers do anything about these flies? Well, it seems as though the Bee Lice can absorb the identifying odours of the colony, so to the workers they don't stand out as aliens that need to be dispatched.

Bee Lice also have a singular ability to cling onto their host – the strongest attachment force of any land insect – thanks to the extraordinary complexity of their feet. Each foot is tipped with comb-like claws and a pair of bristly pads. The claws latch on to the bee's fur, while the bristly pads adhere to its smooth surfaces using a mechanism akin to that seen on gecko's feet. With a simple twisting motion of the foot, the tenacious grip is broken, allowing the fly to scuttle at speed across the bee. This cling factor has true biomimetic potential.

WALLACE'S GIANT BEE

lfred Russel Wallace is most famous for playing second fiddle to Charles Darwin in the double act who brought the idea of evolution by natural selection to the world. Wallace, unlike Darwin, was not independently wealthy, but through his long years in far-flung places he came to the same conclusions as Darwin on the process responsible for the glorious diversity of living things. The enormity of this idea is hard to overstate. Indeed, as biologist Theodosius Dobzhansky wrote: 'Nothing in biology makes sense except in the light of evolution.'

Apart from giving humanity this beautiful framework for understanding life, Wallace was, first and foremost, an indefatigable naturalist and collector. He spent four years in the Amazon but lost nearly two years' worth of specimens when he was shipwrecked. Undeterred, he then set off for Southeast Asia and spent no less than eight years exploring the Malay Archipelago.

He paid a small army of locals to collect wonderful specimens for him. After eight years of scampering around with insect nets and lots of shooting, Wallace had amassed an embarrassment of anecdotes and more than 125,000 specimens, one of which was an enormous bee four times bigger than a worker honeybee: *Megachile pluto*, the largest bee species in the world. He remarks on this species in his book, *The Malay Archipelago*: 'a large black wasp-like insect, with immense jaws like a stag-beetle.' Like most of his specimens, it was collected by a local, their name lost to history, who was paid to find interesting specimens for this tall, bearded white man. That was in 1858 on the island of Bacan and the bee was not seen again for another 123 years.

Then, in 1981, Adam Messer rediscovered this missing bee on Bacan and the surrounding islands, recording some aspects of its ecology. Like all bees, it is the females that do all the hard work of making a nest and rearing a brood. They excavate their nests in the mounds of arboreal termites, using tree resin harvested with their prodigious mandibles to water- and termite-proof their nest tunnels. It is only their size that enables this harvesting. Apart from a single specimen collected in 1991, the species was not seen again until 2018, but this time two specimens, caught by locals, turned up for sale online.

In 2019, Clay Bolt and Eli Wyman searched for the species and eventually found and obtained the first footage of the living bee. This is a big insect with very specific habitat requirements, so its populations are probably rather small and acutely vulnerable. Deforestation and the collection of specimens for sale to collectors are pressing threats to the continued existence of this impressive bee, but at the time of writing, it still has no formal protection. Even with formal protection, unscrupulous dealers have no trouble getting insects like this to people who wish to add them to their collection.

MEGACHILE PLUTO ⊢————————————————⊣ INDONESIA

FAIRY WASP

Late afternoon in a summer meadow humming with life. What look like motes of dust, backlit by the sun, skitter this way and that in the air. Look closer. The particles are actually animals: Fairy Wasps (*Mymaridae*) and their kin, to be precise. These remarkable beings are among the smallest animals, smaller even than some single-celled organisms. Several individuals of the smallest species could fit inside this full stop. Even the heftiest ones are on the cusp of what we can see with the naked eye. For me, they are among the most beguiling of insects and much of their biology is still a mystery.

These tiny insects are masters of miniaturization, squeezing a mind-boggling amount of biological complexity into a tiny space. They have a gut, muscles, reproductive organs, the equivalent of kidneys, an immune system, a system of breathing tubes for the transport of gases and much more besides. At this minute scale, air is as viscous as water and Fairy Wasps scull through it rather than fly, on wings that have evolved into hair-fringed paddles. Their behavioural repertoire is as complex as much larger insects. They seek out and choose their mates and their prey, they groom themselves and avoid danger, responding to the information from their senses that is processed in a brain made up of only around 8,000 neurons. For contrast, there are about 850,000 neurons in a honeybee's brain. Fairy Wasp nerve fibres are so tiny that they likely work differently to normal nerve fibres, i.e. relaying electrical signals. Instead, they may simply work mechanically, pulling on a muscle to get it to contract or relax. These brains might be minuscule, but they will inspire advances in artificial intelligence and robotics.

How is this extreme miniaturization possible? The secret is in the extreme shrinking of cells. This often means getting rid of the cell's nucleus, which takes up a lot of space. The nucleus is present as the cells develop, but in maturity it's broken down, so the cells can get really small.

Why are they so tiny though? What are the benefits of extreme miniaturization? Imagine a habitat. A forest, a meadow, a suburban garden. The size of an animal dictates the space it requires and where and how it can live – the niches. Miniaturization allows animals to exploit spaces and ways of living that larger animals cannot. In the case of the Fairy Wasps and their relatives, shrinking allowed them to take advantage of a bounteous source of prey – the eggs of other insects and spiders. That's right: as benign and delicate as these tiny animals look, they're actually predators, parasitoids to be exact. Parasitoids, unlike parasites, consume their host.

At this minute scale, air is as viscous as water and Fairy Wasps scull through it rather than fly …

The female Fairy Wasp seeks out the eggs of her host, guided by specific odours, and uses her hypodermic needle-like ovipositor to deposit her own egg or eggs inside. Her offspring hatch and go to work on the host embryo, consuming it greedily in its entirety. The fully grown wasp larvae pupate in the eggshell and the new adult Fairy Wasps chew an exit hole in the egg to make their escape. Depending on the species in question, this whole cycle can be completed in a few days.

Fairy Wasps might be tiny, but it's difficult to overstate just how important they and other tiny parasitoid wasps are in terrestrial ecosystems. Any insect or spider you care to mention is targeted and consumed by these wasps, so they're crucial in regulating the populations of their hosts. Their unerring ability to locate and dispatch their hosts is even harnessed by farmers who release them in glasshouses and the like to control pest insects that would otherwise devastate their crops.

Although most people will not have heard of, let alone seen, these tiny beings, rest assured that you're never more than a couple of feet from one. They exist in profusion. Run an insect net through a field for a couple of minutes and you'll catch thousands. Examine your windowsill with a magnifying glass and you'll find a few. Taking time to notice the extraordinary world of miniature beings that surround us alters our appreciation of the world for the better.

FAIRY WASP

Fairy Wasps are among the smallest animals, smaller even than many single-celled organisms.

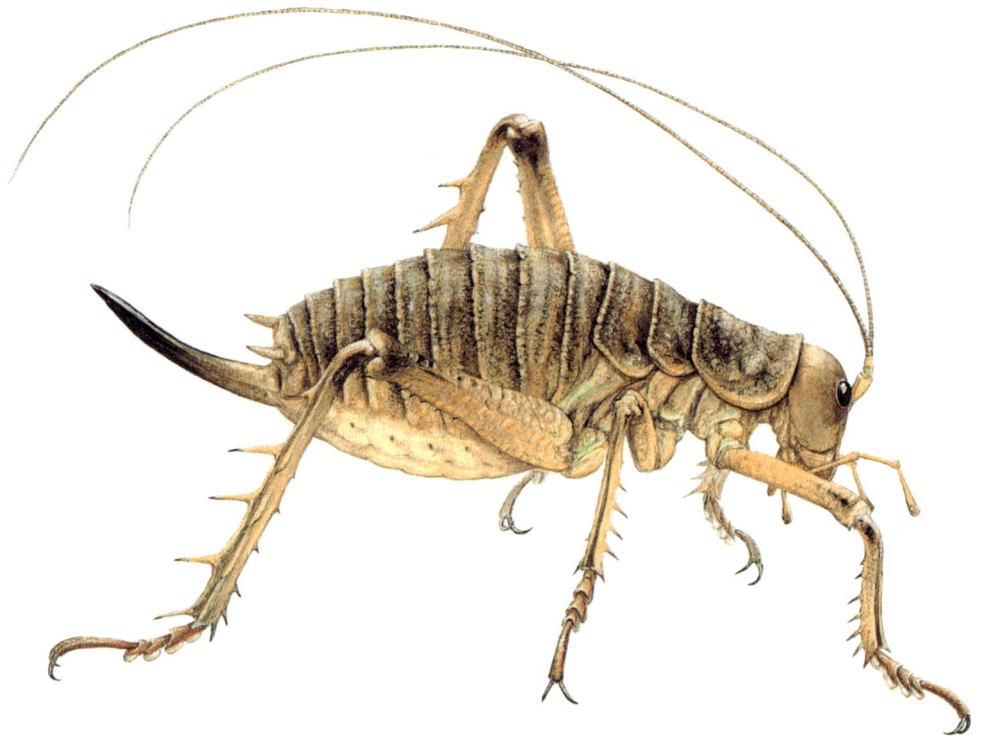

DEINACRIDA HETERACHANTHA ⊢————————⊣ NEW ZEALAND

WĒTĀPUNGA

This enormous, spiky brute is a type of Wētā, basically enormous crickets found only in New Zealand which evolved to fill niches occupied by small rodents in other parts of the world. The Wētāpunga is the largest of these, with a body measuring up to 10 cm and weighing in at up to 70 g – making it one of the heaviest living insects. A nocturnal, nomadic herbivore, the Wētāpunga leaves its daytime refuge to feed on foliage in the canopy. As it's wingless, it must clamber to the tree-tops using its long, strong legs. The allure of pheromones and stridulation brings the sexes together, the females eventually descending to the ground to deposit their eggs into the soil. The name, literally translated from the Te Reo Māori, means the 'god of ugly things', so it seems the first New Zealanders didn't think much of these insects.

New Zealand, like so many other remote archipelagos the world over, is something of an evolutionary laboratory, once part of an ancient southern landmass that was slowly torn asunder by immense, irrepressible geological forces. These constituents drifted and morphed over time to become the continents and islands of the southern hemisphere we know today.

As New Zealand became ever more isolated, its complement of passengers evolved along interesting trajectories. Rather than mammals being the dominant large animals, birds ruled the roost, the largest and most conspicuous of which were the Moa. Scurrying around the feet of these giants and among the trees were insects that had also taken advantage of the dearth of land mammals. Sadly, the first humans who found New Zealand wasted no time in running amok, cutting and burning the forests, scoffing what animals they could, thus driving many of the unique species to extinction. Moa, being large and flightless, were among the first casualties of the human onslaught, hunted to extinction, sadly long gone. Many of the special insects remain though … just.

The seafaring peoples who settled the scattered islands of the South Pacific were an ingenious, intrepid bunch. As well as their intellect, they brought livestock, seeds and stowaways, such as rats – which found the giant crickets rather moreish and ate these large, sluggish and flightless insects very nearly to extinction (see also page 99 – St Helena Giant Earwig). Once abundant through northern New Zealand, these insects had been reduced by the late 19th century to a small population clinging to existence on Te Hauturu-o-Toi (Little Barrier Island). Rats had also reached this island, so without action the Wētāpunga was doomed.

Conservationists set about trying to stop this gradual slide towards oblivion. By eradicating the rats on the island and establishing a captive breeding programme, the fortunes of the Wētāpunga were reversed. Today, more than 5,000 of these impressive insects have been introduced to a number of predator-free islands off the coast of northern New Zealand.

GIANT TIMBER FLY

remember reading about the Giant Timber Flies as a bespectacled student, enthralled and desperate to see one in the flesh. I only had to wait about 20 years. At a research station in Costa Rica, I finally spotted a live one – a *Pantophthalmus* species, high up on a beam in one of the station buildings.

Approaching 5 cm long, so that it would span your palm, these are disconcertingly large flies, on a par with those giant rubber flies you see in toy shops. They are among the largest flies, certainly the bulkiest, and although they look a bit like giant horse flies, they are actually more closely related to soldier flies. The adults have mouthparts for dabbing at liquids, but it's debatable how much they use them because they don't live very long as mature insects. The head, especially in the males, is basically a pair of enormous eyes, primarily for finding females, although nothing is known about their courtship.

The enormous grubs, equipped with impressive mandibles, live in wood. Precious little is actually known about them either. They excavate horizontal galleries that, depending on the species, are in healthy, moribund or fallen trees. Exactly what the larvae are eating is not clear. It has been suggested they have a preference for tree species that produce latex or gloopy sap, and it is this material, fermented by microbes, that they consume. Some entomologists have reported finding host trees peppered with the burrows of hundreds of these larvae, the collective munching and rasping of which can be heard from several metres away.

When fully grown, which might take anywhere between five months and just over two years, the larvae pupate in their burrows. Just before metamorphosis is complete, the pupae wriggle part way out of their burrows to facilitate the escape of the adults. Twenty species of these timber flies are known, all of which are from Central and South America. The adults of many species are attracted to light, but even then they're only rarely seen, which suggests they're rather short-lived. There are undoubtedly more species out there.

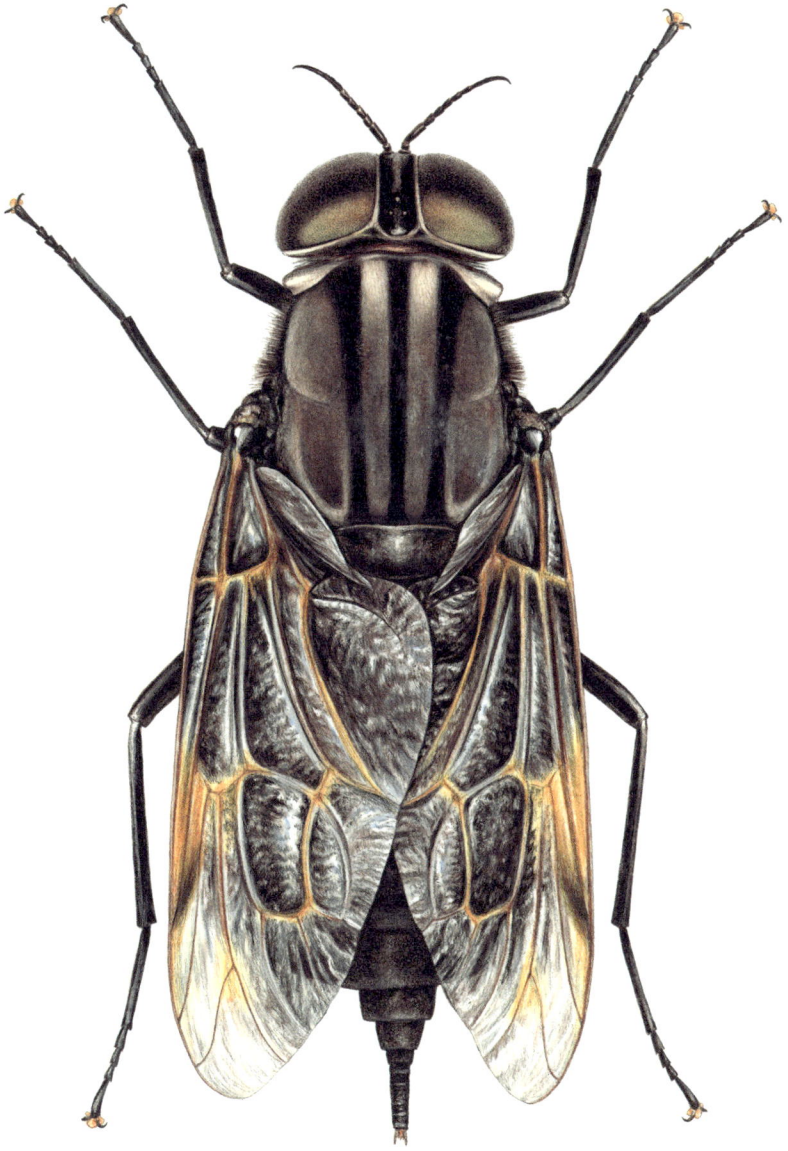

GYROSTIGMA RHINOCERONTIS ├─────────────────────────────┤ AFRICA

RHINOCEROS BOTFLY

Many people will find parasites quite appalling, but this is because they don't know enough about them. The adaptations required to get onto or into a host and to feed there, in many cases to remain and thrive there, are nothing short of mind-boggling, a fascinating window into the blind power of evolution.

An object lesson in just how wonderfully bizarre parasites can be is the Rhinoceros Botfly. With a body 4 cm long and a wingspan of around 7 cm, this is one of the largest fly species in Africa, yet it is also one of the most rarely collected. Rhinoceroses are large and have a reputation for being bad-tempered. Poking around one of these potentially irate ungulates in the wild, looking for flies, perhaps even swishing an insect net around its face, would be a sure-fire way to get its dander up. This is one reason why so few of these flies have been collected.

The other reason is the extremely odd biology of this fly. Its niche is about as niche as it's possible to be, for it spends most of its life attached to the stomach lining of a rhinoceros. How does it even get there? Well, you'd assume the fly's eggs might be somehow consumed by the rhino, perhaps attached to the vegetation they graze and browse. That would be the straightforward way. Instead, the female fly deposits her oblong eggs in the fissured hide near the rhino's horn or elsewhere on the head. The larvae, when they hatch, crawl inside the host via its mouth or nostrils, eventually ending up in its stomach where they embed themselves, head-down in the lining, anchored in place with mouth-hooks and spines. Here, they gorge on the lining, blood and mucus until mature and ready to pupate. Within the host, the larvae can be extremely numerous – hundreds, even thousands strong – and to leave the rhino, they must relinquish their grip and go with the flow to the light at the end of the long, sinuous tunnel – the anus. Deposited in a pile of dung, the fat larvae must work quickly to avoid the many predators in the outside world. They tunnel down through the dung to pupate in the relative safety of the soil. Six weeks later, the adults emerge to begin the cycle again.

Like so many other rarely seen insects, the adult fly's mouthparts are useless, and the energy stores it accumulated as a grub will last it for only three to five days. This fleetingly short adult lifespan is the main reason they are so rarely collected, although the precipitous decline of rhinos is not helping their cause. Indeed, two other close relatives of this fly, one a parasite of the Black Rhinoceros, the other a parasite of the Sumatran Rhinoceros, have not been seen since 1961 and 1884, respectively.

AUSTRALIAN GIANT WOOD MOTH

ragonfly, Dobsonfly, Mantisfly, Plant Louse and Bee Louse. These are well-used names but, like so many other English common names for insects, rather confusing because none of these is an actual fly or a louse. What we need are good, honest and reliable common names for insects. Look no further than the common name for this species. It is a moth, it is a giant and it is found in Australia, so it is called the Australian Giant Wood Moth, or *Endoxyla cinereus*.

Although impressive, the 23 cm wingspan is not the largest of any moth, but it more than makes up for that with its heft – egg-laden females can weigh 30 g, which makes it the heaviest moth on the planet by quite some margin. For comparison, this is about the same weight as a sparrow. Regardless of its size, it is rarely seen, and it remains one of Australia's most enigmatic insects.

It is found throughout eastern, southern and south-western Australia, but the proclivity of the larvae for tunnelling into smooth bark Eucalyptus trees, often damaging them, puts it at odds with the wood-pulp industry. Plantations of any sort are alien – flying in the face of the true essence of natural systems that are by nature busy, complex and messy. It has become clear this moth is a key component – perhaps even an ecosystem engineer – of the sparse forests in which it is found. An ecosystem engineer is any species that changes the structure of a habitat to provide lots of niches for other species – just think of elephants pushing over trees or beavers building dams.

When fully grown, the caterpillar of the Giant Wood Moth can be up to 15 cm long, so it makes a considerable excavation into its host tree, consisting of a feeding chamber and a vertical tunnel into which it retreats when resting, shedding its exoskeleton or pupating. Obviously, this doesn't do the tree much good.

The caterpillar activity weakens the trunk and permits the entry of fungi and bacteria, further compromising the tree until it might eventually split. Moribund and collapsed trees create a more open, structurally complex woodland that benefit this species and lots of others. Not only that, but the vacated cavities are also used by a range of other species, including lorikeets and frogs.

One of Australia's most enigmatic insects.

It might take as long as three years for the caterpillar to grow sufficiently to transform into the adult moth. The adults, when they finally emerge, are bereft of mouthparts, so they can't feed even if they wanted to. Instead, they rely on the stores of fat laid down during their eating marathon as caterpillars, but this gives them only a few days, just enough time for the males and females to find each other and mate. The female deposits as many as 18,000 eggs and it is thought the tiny caterpillars, when they hatch, disperse by ballooning – an incredible phenomenon. The caterpillar extrudes a long filament of silk from its salivary glands which gets long enough to pull the animal into the air via electrostatic repulsion.

As well as being ecosystem engineers, the caterpillars of the Giant Wood Moth and its relatives were an extremely important food source to Indigenous Australians; collectively known as 'witchetty grubs', these grubs have unique names depending on the region and culture. To locate and harvest these caterpillars requires a deep understanding of exactly how and where they live – yet another demonstration of the intimate connection between Indigenous Peoples and their environment, much of which has been sadly lost.

AUSTRALIAN GIANT WOOD MOTH

The extremely short-lived adults of this species are the heaviest moths. As caterpillars they play an important role in the ecosystem.

FEATHERWING BEETLE

As exotic and otherworldly as these insects look, I guarantee that they'll be somewhere near you, while you're reading this. Wherever I look for insects, whether in my garden or the forests of Peru, I find Featherwing Beetles (*Ptiliidae*) in profusion. Most people won't have seen or noticed these beings because they're tiny. I could drop a load of them onto a sheet of white paper right in front of you, and all you would see would be a bunch of what looked like animated full stops, careering in every direction across the paper.

Among the most diminutive insects, the smallest of them are a mere 0.3 mm long. Their common name is derived from the structure of their wings, which are feather-like, fringed with long bristles, very similar to those of the other Lilliputian insects – Fairy Wasps (see page 82). At the scale of these insects, the air is viscous, so their movement through it is more like swishing than flying, hence the heavily modified wings.

Becoming this small has necessitated other changes too, such as reduction and even complete loss of certain organs. In some other tiny beetles, the head simply doesn't have the space to house the brain, so it's been relocated to the thorax, which would be like your brain being in your chest.

Even though some bits of anatomy have been reduced or dispensed with in these tiny insects, the eggs and sperm can be miniaturized only so far. Both types of cell require a nucleus, which takes up lots of space, while the egg must also contain yolk to fuel the developing embryo. This has created a bizarre situation where these tiny insects produce relatively enormous eggs and sperm.

The eggs are half the length of the female and produced one at a time, while, in some species, each individual sperm is longer than the adult beetle. In some Featherwing Beetle species, the very long sperm may function as a mating plug, blocking up a female's reproductive tract and preventing other males from successfully mating with her. Other species produce tailless and therefore immobile sperm. Exactly what these do is anyone's guess, but perhaps they too function as a chastity bung. We just don't know. The sex-lives of these tiny beetles, as with so much else of their biology, is poorly known.

Miniaturization does come at a price, but it is a successful strategy. Featherwing Beetles and a constellation of other tiny insects are found in huge numbers in just about any habitat, where they seek out and abound in decaying organic matter, consuming this material and providing food for a range of larger arthropods.

LABIDURA HERCULEANA   ⊢————————————————⊣   ST HELENA

ST HELENA GIANT EARWIG

St Helena, the tiny, remote island in the South Atlantic, is most well known as the place where Napoleon met his end, banished there after his defeat at Waterloo. Less well known is that, like isolated islands the world over, St Helena was home to a number of endemic species, many of which have gone the same way as the dodo.

To me, the most enigmatic member of St Helena's vanished fauna is the Giant Earwig (*Labidura herculeana*). Compared with other earwigs, this really is a monster, with a total length of around 80 mm, a good proportion of which comprise the curved pincers that characterize this group of insects. I wanted to include this species because there's an outside, though diminishing, chance it might be clinging on somewhere on the island. If the Lord Howe Island Stick Insect could literally cling onto existence on the vertiginous sides of Ball's Pyramid, I live in hope that this extraordinary insect is still out there.

Even though this is a substantial insect, precious little is known about it. First described in 1798, it was more or less forgotten until the 1960s, when a number of individuals were discovered living under boulders in an area known as Horse Point Plain. Exactly how it lived is a mystery, but like other earwigs it was probably omnivorous, and the females were very probably dedicated parents, caring for the eggs and hatchlings. Living individuals, as well as fragments of dead specimens, indicate this monster earwig was found across a swathe of the island, from gumwood forests to seabird colonies. Apparently, they spent most of their time in deep burrows, only venturing out to feed at night after rain.

The extreme size of this earwig is an example of the island effect, an intriguing phenomenon where a species that colonizes an island becomes much larger or smaller than its mainland relatives. Isolated on St Helena for countless generations, free from the depredations of birds and mammals, the Giant Earwig dispensed with flight and grew enormous compared with its mainland relatives. In terms of how it fitted into the ecology of St Helena, it probably had a role similar to small rodents on the mainland.

It's a cruel irony, then, that this Giant Earwig should be decimated by the very animals it was living like. Rodents – specifically rats and mice – inadvertently introduced by sailors stopping off at St Helena, made short work of the flightless earwigs and lots of other species besides. Other introduced species, such as the opportunistic centipede *Scolopendra morsitans*, probably also radically reduced their number.

The gumwood forests have long since gone, the boulders on Horse Point Plain were removed for construction and the seabird colonies are no more, but let's hope this extraordinary species is still clinging on somewhere and that we can understand more about how it lives.

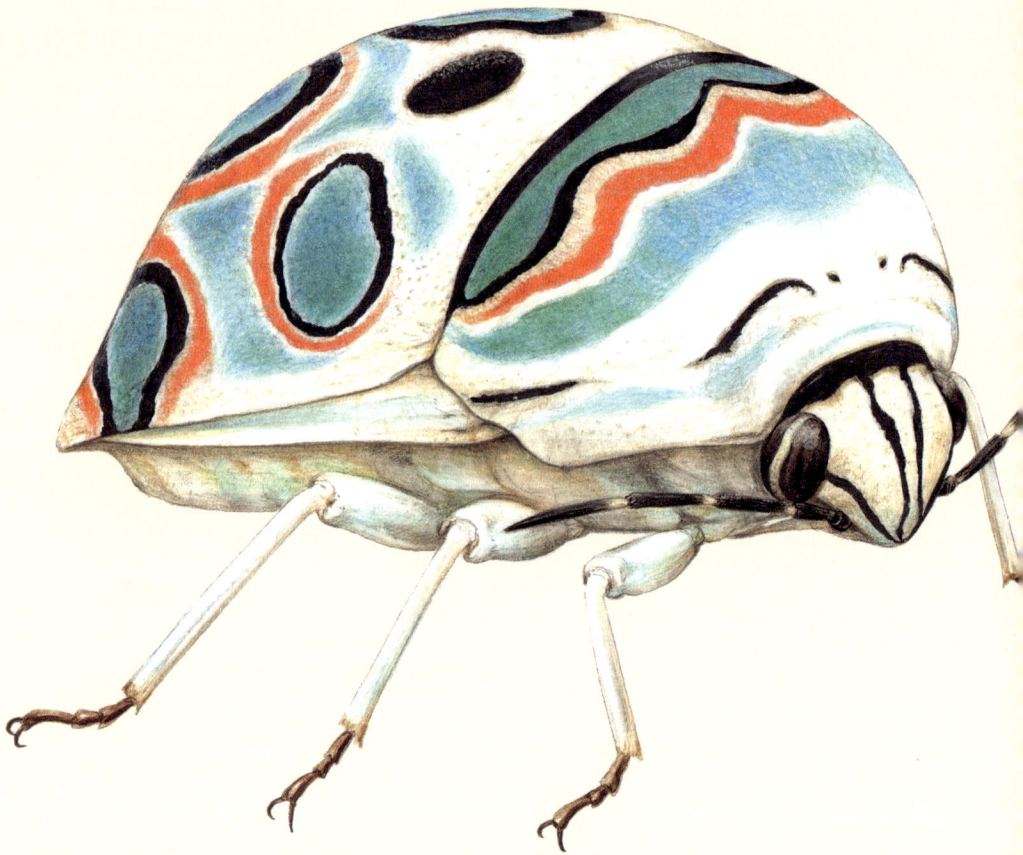

PATTERN

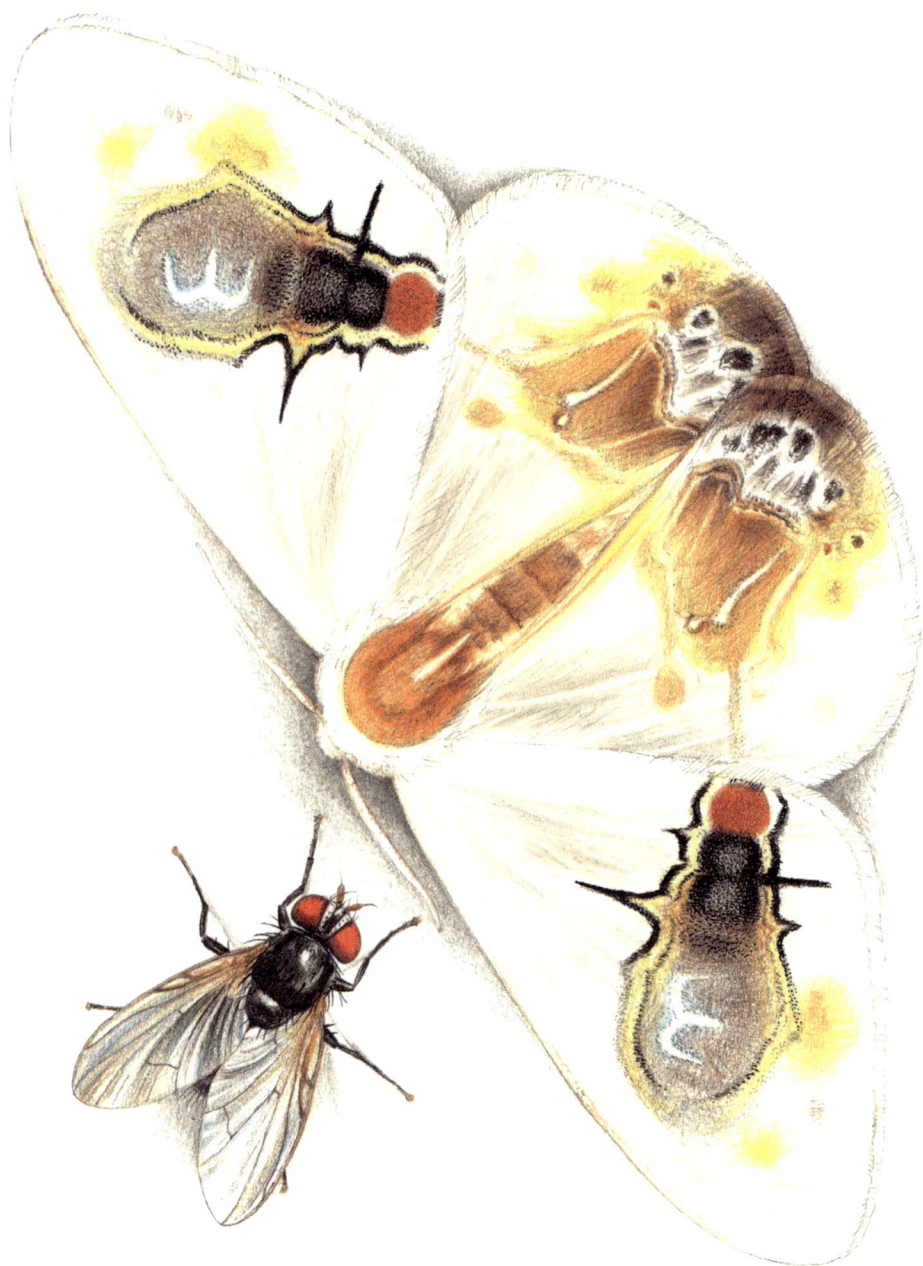

MACROCILIX MAIA ├─────────────────┤ SOUTH ASIA & SOUTHEAST ASIA

BIRD-DROPPING MOTH

Droppings and dung won't be popular fancy-dress themes any time soon, but in the world of insects, pretending to be something that has come out of the digestive tract of another animal is surprisingly common. Birds and mammals have to be pretty desperate to consider eating such things, so faeces are a good thing to pretend to be. Perhaps one of the finest bird-poo mimics is the moth *Macrocilix maia*. Found in India, through some parts of Southeast Asia and into the Far East, this rather rare moth is a beautiful example of mimicry.

The white wings with brown splodges are a convincing impression of bird droppings, but look a bit closer and you'll see that two of those splodges on the forewings have been tweaked by natural selection to resemble a pair of flies that look to be feeding from the large brown splodge on the hind wings. These 'flies' have eyes, thorax, legs and wings. Not only that, but the disguise is topped with a pungent odour that is said to resemble actual bird droppings. The presence of these 'flies' and the odour enhance the overall effect and increase the chances that a keen-eyed predator will be duped by the disguise.

Patterns like this would have prompted lots of head-scratching among early naturalists. Indeed, as the great evolutionary biologist Theodosius Dobzhansky wrote in 1973, 'Nothing in biology makes sense except in the light of evolution.' Without any understanding of evolution by natural selection, the natural world is full of structures that look to have been designed by a Higher Being. Look at these structures again, however, and think about time, the countless generations and the subtle variation within a population – and it's not difficult to grasp how they are the product of evolution by natural selection.

Imagine an ancestral population of this moth. With the exception of one individual, they all have white wings dotted with a few small brown marks. A chance mutation in the aberrant individual means the brown marks on its wings are much bigger and it looks a bit more like a bird dropping than the others. As its disguise is better, it survives and passes on its traits to its offspring. Any variation that improves the chances of survival is more likely to be passed on.

Natural selection often works at quite a slow pace, but in some circumstances, it can happen before our very eyes. The Peppered Moth is one of the best examples of this. The air pollution of the Industrial Revolution left soot deposits on buildings and trees. At this point, Peppered Moths with pale wings began to stand out like sore thumbs. A single mutation caused the moth to be dark rather than pale and the dark form blended in much better on the dark, sooty surfaces. These darker versions survived more often to see another day, and the species tended towards dark morphs. The Clean Air Act in the 1950s actually reversed this trend: the trees became cleaner and thus lighter, and the moth followed suit. Today, there are more light Peppered Moths than dark ones.

STONE-MIMICKING GRASSHOPPER

nhabiting the arid lands of southern Africa are an abundance of species adapted to these dry conditions. One of the most extraordinary of these is the Stone-mimicking Grasshopper which, as you can imagine, is pretty hard to spot. These are very chunky grasshoppers, up to 50 mm in length, but their overall shape, subtle patterns and surface texture make them beautifully camouflaged. In the places where they live, small rocks litter the surface, and the grasshopper blends in with these.

Obviously, this wouldn't be very effective if the grasshopper was bouncing around the whole time, so they sit motionless. This is quite a risky strategy. These are big, juicy grasshoppers – a significant meal and source of moisture for many of the predators that eke out a living in these parched places. Unlike most other grasshoppers, they are flightless, so the quality of their disguise is all they really have. Like all grasshoppers, their bulging back legs allow them to jump, but to do this would demonstrate to an approaching predator that what they thought was a stone is actually dinner.

The populations of this grasshopper vary in appearance, depending on what stones are present. In some areas they've evolved to mimic small chunks of whitish quartz, while in other areas they've had to blend in with a substrate or reddish or dark rocks. This begs the question: is this just one species with a number of different morphs, or a number of distinct, reproductively isolated populations – 'species' in the common parlance?

This is a tricky question and there's no clear-cut answer. We have to remember that the concept of a species is a useful tool, but one that we invented. Our minds thrive on order, and we seek this when making sense of the natural world, but nature is dynamic with poorly defined boundaries. The most widely used definition of a species is based on Ernst Mayr's biological species concept: 'Species are groups of actually or potentially interbreeding natural populations, which are reproductively isolated from other such groups.' This is well known and has some intuitive appeal, but it's very limited and is biased towards animals. Regardless of the organisms in question, species and the lineages they form are continually splitting and rejoining over time, rather like the braided flow of a river in a delta, which is perhaps the best way to visualize what is going on.

With respect to whether the grasshopper is one or several species, no one has done the research to find out. We will need to sequence the DNA of individuals from the different populations, while also looking at exactly how and where the populations live. Combine all of this with their physical characteristics, and we will be able to say whether the groups are sufficiently distinct to be called species.

ALDER MOTH

The odds of any one caterpillar reaching adulthood and fluttering off as a moth or butterfly are vanishingly small. If the parasitoid wasps or flies don't get you, the birds will. To our feathered friends, caterpillars are the cocktail sausages of the insect world. A Blue Tit chick needs as many as 100 caterpillars poked into its waiting maw every day. A single nest may contain 16 chicks! The beleaguered parents of these chicks probably hold their heads in their wings, lamenting their life choices and wondering why they got into a relationship in the first place.

In response to this unrelenting predation pressure, caterpillars have evolved plenty of tricks to get them through to adulthood. Disguise or advertise, that is the question. Many butterfly and moth caterpillars opt for the former – pretending to be an inanimate object, such as a leaf, twig or bird poo. As well as looking like a turd, some species even smell like one too. In stark contrast, lots of species stick out like a sore thumb – broadcasting their toxicity or the fact they taste disgusting to potential predators with bright colours and patterns. There are also plenty of non-toxic or perfectly nice-tasting species that mimic species that are chemically protected

The Alder Moth is interesting because it uses both of these strategies at different times in its life. This species is found across a large swathe of Europe and Asia, where the caterpillars feed greedily on the foliage of several tree species, especially alder and birch. For much of its life, the caterpillar does a pretty good impression of bird poo, but during the transition into the last stage of its caterpillar it opts for a completely different outfit. Gone is the bird-poo disguise, and in its place is a classic warning signal of bold black and yellow stripes. Like so many other insects, Alder Moth caterpillars use plant defences to their own advantage, extracting noxious chemicals from the plants they eat and assimilating them into their own tissues, even modifying them to make them even more noxious. It is these chemicals the caterpillar's bright colours are broadcasting.

Even though the young Alder Moth caterpillars put off predators with their turdish appearance, they are also loaded with toxins and unpalatable to birds. Why then is there such a dramatic change in appearance? As the caterpillars grow, they become more active, culminating in the long march that will take them from the foliage of the trees to deadwood on the ground where they will pupate. The poo disguise only really works when they're not moving around much, so as they become more active, they must resort to warning off predators by advertising how bad they taste.

JEWEL BEETLE

Relatively few people will have knowingly seen a jewel beetle (*Bupres-tidae*), even though there are 15,000 species of them. The largest species are 7 to 8 cm long and they're found on every continent, except Antarctica. Many of them are truly gorgeous, hence the common name, but their looks have been something of a downfall because many of them are coveted by museums, private collectors and even just people who like shiny things.

Aesthetics to one side for a moment, their biology is very interesting. The larvae of some jewel beetles feed on living wood, roots, stems or even within leaves as leaf-miners. Most of them, however, feed on dead or decaying wood, a habitat that is a treasure trove of beetle diversity and is the place to spend time looking if you want to see a lot of beetles. In fact, one of these deadwood jewel beetles possibly holds the record for the longest larval stage of any insect – a whopping 51 years, although some entomologists have scoffed at that figure. The quality of the wood they're munching affects how long the larvae take to get big enough to pupate. In normal situations this might be a few years, depending on the species, but if the wood is dry and poor quality, it will take those larvae much longer to bulk up to the required size.

The requirement for optimal wood in larval development has driven the evolution of some superb adaptations in some of these beetles, perhaps the most intriguing of which is the ability to detect forest fires at long range. *Melanophila* jewel beetles have a pair of small pits on their thorax, which are loaded with sensory organs that detect infrared radiation, allowing them to home in on forest fires. This might seem like an odd superpower. Flying towards a raging inferno without the intention of putting it out may seem like a peculiar strategy destined to end badly. The truth is that the larvae of these species find optimal conditions for development in freshly burnt wood, hence the need to head towards fires.

These beetles are so colourful and glittery … they've made their way into fashion.

Back to their appearance. These beetles are so colourful and glittery (including *Chrysochroa fulgens*, pictured) that they've made their way into fashion. In Central and South America, the elytra, or hardened forewings, of some of the large species are made into jewellery and adorn clothes and textiles, a custom that began with the Indigenous Peoples of those places. In India, mainly Rajasthan and Uttar Pradesh, small pieces of these beetles' elytra were used like sequins in the type of embroidery known as *gota patti*. Clothing, turbans, jewellery and even the paintings of the Mughal era were adorned with this embroidery, and it continued to be used into the Victorian era.

The colours and patterns of many of the jewel beetles are simply stunning, but what are they for? The colours we see are a result of structural colouration (see the Blue Morpho – page 14) and they may help to camouflage these beetles from their main predators – birds. Some of the larger species that are patterned with large white spots or bands are very difficult to spot when they're resting on a sun-dappled tree trunk or branch. Another possibility is that the bold patterns broadcast the toxicity of these beetles to hungry predators: many of them are known to be loaded with unique bitter toxins, known as buprestins. Others may simply be lying about their toxicity, mimicking other species that are chemically defended.

The colours and patterns of these beetles advertise toxins and may also serve as camouflage on sun-dappled tree trunks and branches.

ROVE BEETLE

A close look at the body of this rove beetle reveals the pattern on its surface to be reminiscent of the Thing from the Fantastic Four. The intricate sculpted surface of this beetle's exoskeleton is all about protection, for it lives only with army ants. A strange choice, I know. Army ants are not widely regarded as welcoming bedfellows – far from it. They wander the forest floor of the Neotropics in streaming columns, seizing and dismembering any small animals they can catch. Unlike other ants, they do not make a permanent nest either, instead forming a structure – a bivouac – from their own bodies in which they shelter the queen and nurture the brood.

This doesn't sound like much of a welcoming niche – and, on the face of it, it's not – but there are a number of enticements. The internal complexity of the temporary nests and the bounty of food and protection they offer has been a draw for a menagerie of other animals. Some of these are completely dependent on the army ants, some live in close proximity to them, others live in the nests but are not tolerated if discovered, and there are still more that fool the ants and are integrated nearly seamlessly into the colony. In a recent study in Costa Rica, the roll call of dependents living with six species of army ant was 62 species, including 49 beetles, 11 flies, one millipede and one silverfish. Fourteen of these were new to science!

This interesting rove beetle (*Ecitonides constanceae*) is one such species and one that is also new to science. During an expedition to the Amazon of southern Peru, it was drawn to a light trap I was using to attract insects. Incidentally, we named it after my daughter. She was underwhelmed, but she'll appreciate the significance of this as she gets older. Hopefully. Most rove beetles can fly, their wings folded ingeniously beneath the very short elytra, and this one was obviously on the wing, probably on its way to find an army ant nest. To date, this is the eighth species known from this genus and they all live with army ants. Exactly how they live is unknown. The brush of what look like hairs on the tip of its abdomen are called trichomes. In other beetles that live with ants, these trichomes provide a greater surface area for the wafting of pheromones that mimic those of the ants, allowing the owner to blend in and not get torn apart like soft bread. The tough, sculpted exoskeleton of the beetle probably provides a bit of protection if the ants smell a rat – well, a beetle pretending to be an ant – that is perhaps too near the most sensitive parts of the nest. After all, the ant/interloper relationship is another example of an evolutionary arms race – the ants want to detect undesirables in their nest and the undesirables want to avoid detection.

This rove beetle may prowl the temporary nests, surreptitiously nibbling the ant brood, taking advantage of injured, moribund workers or scouring the nest's refuse piles for edible morsels. As you might imagine, finding these is one thing, but documenting how they live is quite another.

VANESSA CARDUI ├────────────────────────────┤ WIDESPREAD

PAINTED LADY

The movement of animals with the seasons has always been of great interest to people for practical reasons – for example 'Where has all the food gone?' – and spiritual reasons: 'God must be unhappy with us because all the food has gone.' Up until fairly recently, there were some outrageous claims made about this phenomenon. In the 16th century, Swedish priest Olaus Magnus, who may have been taking something, conjectured that swallows hibernate in the mud at the bottom of lakes and streams. In the late 17th century, Charles Morton, an English minister, proposed that birds went to the moon for the winter. The first solid evidence of birds migrating between continents wasn't until 1822, when a stork with an African spear through its neck was found in Germany.

In these more enlightened days, we can probe more deeply into what animals get up to. The movements of many bird species are now well understood, but there is still much more to discover. Many insect species also undertake phenomenal migrations, although it is only in the last couple of decades that we have got more of a handle on their movements.

One of the most remarkable of these is the migration of the Painted Lady butterfly which, as the name suggests, is a beautifully patterned animal. Every year, this species undertakes an enormous migration from Sub-Saharan Africa to the Arctic Circle, a round trip of around 14,000 km. Using vertical-looking radar, it has recently been discovered that these insects fly at heights of 500 m to take advantage of prevailing winds that allow them to fly at speeds of nearly 50 km/h.

What's really interesting is that, typically, it's not individual butterflies doing this journey, but six successive generations tracking the northern temperate summer. Most of the butterflies returning to Africa each autumn are the great-great-great-great grandchildren of the individuals who struck north from Africa earlier in the year.

These animals weigh only a fraction of a gram, and their brain is little bigger than a pinhead, yet they complete this epic journey without the benefit of experience or being able to learn from older, wiser individuals. Their migration is triggered by environmental cues and made possible with their sophisticated compound eyes that work as a sun compass. Their eyes allow them to fly in the correct direction for the northward and southward legs of their journey, based on the position of the sun in the sky, even when it's concealed by cloud. The environmental cue the butterflies mainly rely on is day length, although temperature and the condition of their foodplants may also play a role. When day length is increasing, the caterpillars will develop into butterflies with an unerring urge to travel north. As day length decreases later in the summer, a behavioural switch is flicked, and the caterpillars develop into butterflies who want to fly south. The eyes of Painted Lady butterflies – and indeed most insects – can detect polarized light, enabling them to pinpoint the position of the sun and navigate by it, even when it's concealed.

AMERICAN BURYING BEETLE

This large black beetle with its bold orange markings was once found across a swathe of North America, but it took a population nosedive, disappearing from 90% of its former range, although the work of dedicated conservationists has stemmed this decline. Urbanization and intensive agriculture will have certainly played a part in these beetles' disappearance, but the exact reasons are unclear.

Burying beetles, as their name suggests, are fond of burying things, notably the carcasses of small vertebrates, which they're extremely good at finding. They have to be. Dead animals are attended on their journey back to the soil by a fleet of insects. Flies of various stripes, such as blow flies, deal with the corpse in the early stages of decay. The larvae of these flies – maggots – are corpse-strippers *par excellence*, devouring all the soft tissues in a remarkably short period of time – especially in warm weather. The burying beetles have to get to the carrion before the maggots have got to work. No sooner has the small mammal or bird breathed its last breath than the burying beetles are on its trail, detecting the telltale aroma of death from at least 3 km away and reaching the animal, sometimes within one hour of its demise.

Favoured carrion are those between 80 and 200 g, which will likely attract several of these beetles. Once in attendance, there's a fair bit of hurly-burly, the beetles tussling with each other to take control of the dead creature until only a dominant male and female remain. The clock is ticking, and this pair must work quickly because they can be usurped by others of their species at any point and the carcass will start to rot. Over the course of the next few hours, they work frantically, digging around and under the carcass to bury and conceal it. Once safely squirrelled away under the surface, the happy couple celebrate by mating and then set about excavating a chamber around the corpse.

To prepare the corpse for what's to come, the pair now denude it of its fur or feathers, work it into a ball shape and smear it with secretions from their anal and salivary glands. These secretions are extremely important because they prevent the growth of microbes that would feast on the dead animal. With the carcass now prepared, the female lays her eggs and the couple wait. About six days later, the pair show their tender side as doting parents – a level of care and devotion that is unparalleled among the insects. The parents guide their newly hatched offspring to the carcass, opening up a feeding pit on it and regurgitating food for their waiting brood. At least one parent, sometimes both, will remain with the young, feeding and cleaning them until they're ready to pupate.

NICROPHORUS AMERICANUS ⊢————————⊣ NORTH AMERICA

BEEWOLF

This is a wasp, but not the social, colony-living insect that harasses a picnic or seems intent on drowning itself in a pint of cider. This, like the vast majority of other wasp species, is a solitary hunter. There are approximately 20,000 species of solitary hunting wasps, but the biology of only a handful of those species has been studied in any detail. The Beewolf is one of those species, thanks to the patience and creativity of Erhard Strohm and his colleagues who shone a light on its extraordinary life.

The female Beewolf makes her nest, a gently sloping tunnel in sandy soil that extends for 20–30 cm, off which are anywhere between three and 34 brood chambers, small voids connected to the main tunnel, in which her offspring will develop – one larva to each brood chamber.

The next step is where the Beewolf lives up to its name, for she must hunt honeybees to stock her brood chambers. Patrolling a flower-rich area, the Beewolf spots a honeybee sipping nectar and strikes, grappling it to the ground before using her sting to administer a tiny amount of venom, with surgical precision, into a cluster of nerve cells behind its front pair of legs. Almost immediately, the honeybee's muscles succumb to an irreversible paralysis.

The Beewolf clutches the honeybee to her underside and takes off for her nest, pushing her flight muscles and navigational abilities to the limit. The prey more than doubles the Beewolf's weight and the flight back to the nest – perhaps hundreds of metres or even more than a kilometre – is an extraordinary test of endurance.

Back at her nest, she drags the honeybee into the darkness of the brood chamber and licks it all over, coating it with secretions from special glands in her head, effectively embalming it, filling in every little crack and smoothing out protuberances so there are no focal points for water to condense on. As there's nowhere for condensation to form, the honeybee stays dry and mould-free. Fungi defeated with physics!

When the brood chamber is fully provisioned, which might take as many as six honeybees, the Beewolf lays a single egg. As a parting gift, the Beewolf leaves a blob of white matter from little cavities on her antennae on the interior wall of the chamber before finally sealing it. The parting gift is actually a mass of symbiotic bacteria, called *Streptomyces philanthi*, that live with the Beewolf and nowhere else.

The Beewolf clutches the honeybee and takes off for her nest, pushing her flight muscles to the absolute limit.

The Beewolf grub, when it hatches, makes short work of the paralysed honeybees in its brood cell. In as little as a week, the grub devours the honeybees and is ready to spin a silken cocoon in which it will see out the autumn and winter in a deep sleep. This is where the astonishing functions of the symbiotic bacteria are revealed. Firstly, the little white mass of bacteria functions like an exit sign in the pitch-black of the brood chamber, guiding the position the larva pupates in so that its head faces the main tunnel, ready for when it emerges as an adult the following summer. Correctly positioned, the larva spins its silken cocoon, incorporating some of the symbiotic bacteria as it does so. These turn the cocoon into an antimicrobial fortress by producing compounds which kill harmful bacteria and fungi that might otherwise infest the inactive larvae during the wet, colder months.

BEEWOLF

The females of this wasp go to extraordinary lengths to supply an underground nest with provisions for their larvae.

ZOPHERUS CHILENSIS ├────────┤ SOUTHERN USA &
CENTRAL AMERICA

IRONCLAD BEETLE

Central to the success of the insects is the exoskeleton, a tough, light-weight and waterproof capsule that has enabled these animals to exploit just about every terrestrial and freshwater niche. The beetles, more than any other insects, have really pushed the exoskeleton envelope. In beetles, the first pair of wings have evolved into tough, jointed shells – the elytra – that protect both the delicate hind wings and the abdomen. This innovation allows them to explore and root around in some really desirable habitats, such as rotting plants, soil, carcasses and dung. Crucially, the elytra protect the wings, so the beetles, when in need of mates or a new pile of filth, can simply take to the air.

Not only that, but beetles evolved when things were hotting up, predator-wise. Those Johnny-come-latelies, the vertebrates, wanted a piece of the life-on-land action and were steadily making their presence felt for arthropods who had had the land to themselves for at least 30 million years, namely by scarfing this easy prey. The elytra of beetles gave them a degree of protection from these predators.

The never-ending struggle between predator and prey, as well as the pressure of surviving in hot, arid places, has driven the evolution of perhaps the toughest insect exoskeletons of all – that of the Ironclad Beetles. One of these species, the superbly named Diabolical Ironclad Beetle (*Phloeodes diabolicus*), can withstand a force equivalent to 39,000 times its own weight. Beetle fanciers and museum curators eager to add this species to their collection have to drill a hole in the specimens before they try to poke a pin into them.

The secret behind the extreme strength of the exoskeleton of these beetles has recently been revealed using micro-CT scanning, an imaging technique that uses X-rays to construct a 3D, slice-by-slice model of the insect. It turns out the connection between the elytra, where they touch each other and the abdomen has become a complex joint consisting of interlocking sections that look like the tabs of jigsaw pieces. These tabs and the sockets they lock into are composed of multiple layers, like an onion skin, that separate when the joint is squeezed, thus spreading the forces and preventing the beetle from being crushed. This is yet another example of insect biology that will undoubtedly yield engineering breakthroughs, as mimicking these joints will provide new ways of linking materials with different properties in applications such as aerospace.

The armour of the Ironclad Beetles has come at a cost, though, because the complex joins between the elytra and abdomen has rendered them flightless. Restricted to walking, being rather large and long-lived, these beetles aroused the curiosity of the Mayans who used them as living jewellery, a custom that goes back centuries and is still practised today in some places. Used like an animated brooch, the unfortunate beetle is decorated with semi-precious jewels and tethered to a pin with a small chain.

STINGING LONGHORN BEETLE

Longhorn Beetles, so called because of their extremely long, mobile antennae, are a very large group of insects, composed of more than 35,000 species, with many more out there still to describe. Ranging in size from a little over 2 mm to nearly 170 mm in the Titan Longhorn, they have long been coveted by collectors for their handsome appearance.

In most species, the pallid grubs are wood nibblers, using powerful mandibles to chomp through the tough material and enlisting the help of a whole raft of microorganisms to break down the otherwise indigestible fibres. Their proclivity for wood often puts them at odds with humans, as the larvae of some species can leave the timber of commercially important tree species riddled with feeding tunnels.

In contrast, the adults are often beautifully cryptic, their colours and patterns affording them some protection from their enemies, allowing them to blend in on tree bark mottled by lichen and algae. When this camouflage fails, they rely on other defences, including powerful jaws, sharp spines or noxious chemicals, to nip, prick and irritate would-be predators. Not even jaws, spines and toxins are enough, though, as starkly demonstrated by a large Longhorn Beetle I saw in Peru that had been brutally torn asunder in the trees by an unseen predator. The front part of its body – the well-protected head and thorax, ripped off and cast aside – was crawling pitifully on the ground in front of me, while above me, somewhere in the trees, the abdomen was devoured.

It's very unlikely for a Longhorn Beetle to meet such an ignominious end because it has another way of defending itself: it can sting. Stings are the speciality of scorpions and Hymenoptera – the group of insects that includes wasps, ants and bees. What's really interesting is that this beetle stings with its antennae, both of which are extremely mobile and tipped with sharp points that can be jabbed into an unsuspecting enemy with some force. In humans, the sting of this beetle causes pain and inflammation, but I can imagine that any bird or primate getting jabbed in the face by one of these stingers would drop the beetle with some haste before moving swiftly on.

It's not exactly clear what the sting is injecting to cause this inflammation. Is it a venom produced by the beetle, or something assimilated from the host plants of the larvae as they develop in wood? Some of the relatives of this beetle have been reared from trees that contain irritating saps or resins. An answer to this question may be some time in coming because it's a very rarely seen species, represented by a relatively small number of specimens in museum collections. It is known from Bolivia, Brazil, Paraguay and Peru, but precious little else is known of its biology, particularly the host trees in which the larvae develop.

CICINDELA CHINESIS ⊢————————————————————————⊣ ASIA

CHINESE TIGER BEETLE

Tearing after Tiger Beetles on a sandy path, catching one in my hand and then getting bitten by it, is one of my earliest childhood memories. For anyone who likes insects, Tiger Beetles hold considerable allure, not only for their beauty – many species glitter like jewels in the sunlight – but also because they grab your attention with their frenetic activity. As an adult, I've pursued them, often in vain, across riverbanks in Borneo, deserts in Namibia and Pacific beaches in Costa Rica.

The bulk of the 2,600 or so species are instantly recognizable. Bright colours, bold patterns, long legs and large eyes sitting above fearsome mandibles, such as *Cicindela chinesis*, pictured. Looking at them closely and seeing them in action, there can be no confusion as to their purpose – they are consummate predators, sprinting and periodically taking to the air in pursuit of other insects. Among the insects, their running speed is unequalled – the fastest species cover about 170 body lengths per second, which is equivalent to you or me running at very nearly the speed of sound.

They run so quickly that their visual system can't cope with the blur of the surroundings. Watching them hunt, you will see them stop frequently, which allows them to reorientate themselves to get a fix on their quarry. The prey, once captured, is dispatched by the enormous, sharp mandibles that chomp and pierce its body. Like many other predatory beetles, tiger beetles practise what is known as 'extra-oral', a technical term for what is basically regurgitating digestive fluids over the prey and slurping up the resultant soupy mess.

If anything, Tiger Beetle larvae are even more fascinating than the adults. They, too, are fierce predators, but rather than engaging in active pursuit they specialize in ambush from the mouth of a burrow, excavated typically in the ground, but also in deadwood. A kink in their abdomen equipped with hook-like bristles holds them in position within the lair, and their heavily armoured head is stationed at the mouth of the burrow, jaws agape and waiting for any suitably sized arthropods to wander within range. Beady eyes and sensitive bristles detect a beetle or ant that strays too close to the burrow and, in a flash, the Tiger Beetle larva lunges from its burrow and grabs the doomed prey in its trap-like jaws before retreating downwards into the dark to consume its prize.

As fearsome as Tiger Beetles are, they too have their enemies, among the most beguiling of which is a wingless, parasitoid wasp that baits the beetle larva, encouraging it to lunge from its burrow. The wasp deftly dodges the snapping jaws of the larva, slips into the burrow and delivers a paralysing sting, incapacitating the larva almost immediately. The wasp, only a fraction of the size of the host, drags the Tiger Beetle larva deeper down into the burrow, lays a single egg on it and then seals up the burrow before seeking out another host. The wasp larva eventually hatches and consumes the paralysed beetle larva in its entirety.

SMALL-HEADED FLY

As the old saying goes: 'tired of Small-Headed Flies, tired of life.' Outside entomological circles these are not well-known animals, but they deserve to be – even if just for looks alone. With their comically tiny heads (which are little more than just eyes), hunched backs and dumpy bodies, they have an air of innocence about them – but their cute appearance hides a dark secret. Like so many other insects, they're parasitoids (probably the commonest insect lifestyle), and as larvae they consume spiders from the inside out.

The female fly deposits a batch of eggs on or near a spider's web, which hatch into a number of active larvae. These seek out the host and one of them will win the Small-headed Fly equivalent of the lottery and manage to get inside the unsuspecting spider, often through a leg joint. From there they wriggle to the arachnid's book lung and sit tight, sometimes for years, waiting for the doomed host to grow to a sufficient size. When the time is right, the fly larva somehow manipulates the behaviour of the spider, making it spin a protective web before consuming it.

This way of life can seem ghoulish to us, but the very existence of such animals was a real affront to religiously minded folk of the Victorian era, including Charles Darwin, who just wouldn't accept that a beneficent god would create such things. Along with finches and the riot of life in the Malay Archipelago, I think parasitoids probably played a part in changing Darwin's and Alfred Russel Wallace's worldview, which was eventually articulated as evolution by natural selection. Ecologically speaking, this way of life – the way of the parasitoid – is crucial to the functioning of terrestrial and freshwater ecosystems, such is the abundance and diversity of these insects (see Fairy Wasp – page 82).

Beyond its appearance and nefarious interactions with spiders, the Small-headed Fly depicted here is interesting for another reason – namely its waspish patterning. It's actually a fairly convincing mimic of a Chalcid Wasp – which is also a parasitoid, but of solitary bees rather than spiders. This type of mimicry is known as Batesian mimicry after the 19th-century naturalist and explorer Henry Walter Bates, who journeyed to South America with Wallace and spent 11 years exploring the Amazon and its tributaries.

Batesian mimicry is where a harmless species – in this case the Small-headed Fly – has evolved to imitate the warning signals of a harmful species – in this case, the wasp, which is equipped with a sting. Granted, the fly is not harmless to spiders, but the predators of both of these insects are birds and this signal – the black and yellow warning colouration – is for them. Getting stung in the mouth by one of these wasps etches this warning pattern in the brain of a naïve bird and it will steer well clear of this signal again, even if the owner of the signal is actually harmless.

BEE ROVE BEETLE

n flight, this furry insect, banded in black, yellow and white, looks very much like a bumblebee. Take a closer look, though, and you will see that this is no bee. It is actually a type of rove beetle. We've already been introduced to a couple of these (see pages 65 and 112), but their diversity is staggering. Along with the weevils, rove beetles are the most successful animals on the planet in terms of species and the breadth of where they live. About 68,000 rove beetle species are known, the bulk of which are small, secretive and easily overlooked animals. You can find them in the deepest recesses of ant nests, the rocky shore of the sea and everywhere in between.

Most rove beetles are rather elongated animals with short wing cases – elytra – that leave most of the abdomen uncovered. This adaptation may be key to their success, increasing their flexibility for wriggling through the tiny spaces in the soil, leaf litter and decaying organic matter. Even though their wing cases are normally very small, most of them have fully formed wings and are adept in the air. Deploying the wings in the blink of an eye and getting them back into the incredibly small space under the elytra is a marvel of nature. Muscles, the elastic properties of the wing veins, gyrating the abdomen and some very ingenious folding allows the wings to be quickly stowed. This may inspire new ways of folding and packing the solar-panel arrays of satellites and a number of other everyday applications.

Back down to Earth with a bump, the Bee Rove Beetle, albeit magnificent, is an animal of mammal dung, especially cowpats that have dried up a bit to form a nice crust above a liquid centre. They feed not on the dung, but on the other animals that are drawn to it, specifically the raft of dung beetles that come flocking to tunnel through it, pulling lumps of it down into the ground as food for their offspring. Only active during warm, sunny conditions, this rove beetle is an energetic hunter, pursuing a likely target across the dung and quickly dispatching it by lopping off its head with those powerful mandibles.

In recent decades, it has become the trend to prophylactically treat livestock and, indeed, pets with wormer medication, drugs that are extremely effective and not just against gut parasites. When these drugs end up in the dung of the treated animal, they also kill the insects that depend on the dung, which has caused a free fall in the number of dung beetles, which, in turn, has led to a decline in their predators, such as this species. These dung insects are a vital component of terrestrial ecosystems, and we poison them at our peril. Eliminating these insects disrupts a vital link in the delicately balanced food web.

DEATH'S-HEAD HAWK-MOTH

I f there's one moth species that's firmly embedded in the collective psyche, it must be this one, following an appearance in *The Silence of the Lambs* and on the promotional poster for the film. The insect in the artwork for the film is indeed based on this moth, but, if you look closely, you will see that the skull motif is actually made up of a group of naked human figures – a further reference to the content of the film.

Macabre thrillers to one side, this large moth is fascinating in its own right. Hawk-moths, also known as Sphinx Moths, are elegant, often large moths. With their strong wings and powerful flight muscles they can fly large distances and hover expertly to drink nectar from flowers. Some of them, such as the Hummingbird Hawk-moth are day-fliers. During the COVID lockdowns, with options for amusement limited, moth trapping surged in popularity, in the UK at least. If you've ever seen or done a moth trap yourself, you'll know that finding a hawk-moth or, even better, a bunch of them is always a highlight. Rearing the caterpillars of these animals is even better. Like the adults, the caterpillars are spectacular animals. Hatching from their tiny eggs, the caterpillars are eating machines that grow almost alarmingly fast. In the case of this species, the fully grown caterpillar is a bright yellow sausage of an animal, up to 15 cm long. It will gorge itself on the foliage of a range of plants but is often seen on potatoes.

Three species of Death's-head Hawk-moth are known, ranging from Africa to Asia and northwards into Europe. With climate change, it's very likely this species will become established in regions where it couldn't historically survive. This spread won't be welcomed by beekeepers because these moths have a taste for honey, raiding the nests of honeybees to steal this sweet liquid. It seems, like lots of other nest raiders, Death's-head Hawk-moths mimic the odour of the honeybees, allowing them to wander about the nests, drinking their fill of honey.

[The caterpillars are] veritable eating machines that grow almost alarmingly fast.

The conspicuous markings on their thorax are part of their anti-predator defences. These markings are only faintly skull-like and how they appear to us is more a consequence of our brain being hardwired to see faces wherever we look, from trees to toast and moths. When threatened, the live moth splays its wings, displaying brightly coloured hindwings. When viewed upside down, it has been suggested this display might mimic the face of a much larger animal to startle potential predators. Proving this either way would be quite tricky. The display is enhanced still further when the moth squeaks loudly like a dog's toy, sucking in air and quickly expelling it again to vibrate its mouthparts.

DEATH'S-HEAD
HAWK-MOTH

To startle their enemies, these moths flash their brightly coloured hindwings and emit a loud squeak.

PICASSO BUG

The wild patterns on the back of this true bug have earned it the name Picasso Bug, as some feel the colours and markings channel the work of the Spanish artist. I suppose you can see what you want in these markings, but as is nearly always the case for bright, contrasting patterns in the world of insects, they're a warning to potential predators that the owner is poisonous or venomous or tastes disgusting.

This bug sits in the latter camp. When threatened, it emits a liquid with a strong, noxious odour that only the most desperate, most olfactorily challenged predator would ignore. To our nose, these can actually smell quite sweet – pear-drop sweets are the closest approximation I can come up with. You definitely wouldn't want to eat one though. The secretions of some species can burn, which I learnt the hard way when I handled a related species and inadvertently touched my upper lip. Blisters started to form almost immediately, and I spent the next few minutes dousing the area with water and cursing my stupidity.

Found throughout much of sub-Saharan Africa, the Picasso Bug has chemical defences good enough that it often perches in conspicuous places on its host plants, so other common names have been coined for it, including Zulu Hud Bug and iCikwa in the Zulu language, a reference to its painted appearance.

In this species and its relatives, a shield-like extension of the thorax protects the abdomen and wings, akin to the elytra of beetles. Through their piercing, straw-like mouthparts they drink plant juices. Sap is nutritionally impoverished, so insects that live on this liquid need the help of symbiotic microorganisms. In these bugs, the beneficial microbes are housed within crypts – small sac-like or tubular outgrowths of the gut, where they digest the plant juices and produce the essential nutrients the bug needs. Without these microbes, the bugs cannot survive. Where do they get the microbes from? In many cases, the microbes are transmitted 'vertically' from mother to offspring. The eggs, as they're laid, are coated with microbe-laden secretions that the youngsters imbibe when they hatch, inoculating their own gut with the crucial microbes.

The interactions between gut microbes and animals are very widespread, so it is important to view an individual animal as an ecosystem in its own right. Any animal species is so much more than just the sum of its genome. It is a complex system, an interplay between myriad unicellular organisms and a multicellular organism, the full significance of which we are only just beginning to understand.

LADYBIRD COCKROACH

The relationship between the general public and cockroaches is complicated. On the one hand, most people are appalled by them – even the word itself is an insult. Seeing a cockroach or two in a restaurant is enough to torpedo the reputation of that establishment. Finding cockroaches scuttling for cover when you turn on the lights in a hotel room would not fill you with much confidence about the hygiene standards of the place. On the other hand, we also love to mythologize, formulating strange claims about them based on flimsy bits of scientific evidence – for example, cockroaches are the only animals that can survive without their head, or cockroaches will be the only survivors of a nuclear apocalypse.

Regardless of our disdain for them, the reality is that only about 30 cockroach species are associated with humans and their dwellings. Only a few of these can really be considered to be pests, mainly because they spoil food and can spread pathogenic microbes around. Most people don't realize there are actually around 4,500 cockroach species, spread across the globe, but concentrated in the tropics. Remarkably, sequencing DNA to unravel the evolutionary relationships of living things revealed that termites are extremely specialized, colony-living cockroaches. Ecologically, cockroaches are important animals. Typically, they're ground-dwelling creatures, eager to consume all manner of foodstuffs, thereby recycling organic material and returning energy and nutrients back to the soil.

Among the assembled cockroach ranks there is considerable beauty, especially in the tropical species. This particular species and its relatives share the warning colouration of various beetles. In this case, the cockroach looks like a Ladybird Beetle which broadcasts its toxicity with black spots on an orange background, perhaps the most well-known example of warning colouration there is. When harassed by a naïve predator, such as a bird or mammal, the Ladybird Beetle bleeds colourful blood from its leg joints. The hungry predator is about to learn an important lesson because the blood of these beetles is loaded with toxic alkaloids and foul-smelling compounds. Any predator that tries to eat one of these beetles won't forget the experience in a hurry, and those distinctive warning colours will be etched into its memory.

These cockroaches are chemically defended too, but rather than evolve a completely different warning pattern, natural selection was guided by what warning colours were already present and common in the environment. With even more bearers of the warning knocking about, the chances of predators seeing and learning are increased, improving its overall reach and effectiveness.

EASTER EGG WEEVIL

'm sure you can see where the common name of this weevil comes from. This species and its relatives, about 100 known species in the genus *Pachyrhynchus*, are all exquisite works of nature – their brilliant markings sparkling with every colour of the rainbow. Like in the Blue Morpho (see page 14) and other insects with metallic iridescence, the bright colours of these weevils are structural. The patterns on their body are made up of tiny scales, the microscopic layers catching, enhancing and reflecting certain wavelengths of light that change depending on the angle from which the scales are being viewed. The bright, bold pattern of these weevils is yet another example of warning colouration, a signal to predators that they taste really bad.

As just a sliver of Southeast Asia's embarrassment of entomological riches, these weevils are broadly distributed across this part of the world. Since they are large and completely flightless, it was something of a conundrum how these weevils had populated the islands of Southeast Asia. The adults can store air in the space beneath their fused elytra, so it was thought that perhaps they could survive periods of bobbing about in the sea at the mercy of the currents and winds, eventually making landfall at distant islands. It turns out the adults can survive for only a few hours in seawater, so they must get around another way. The eggs and larvae are more resilient though.

The adult beetles deposit their eggs in various bits of an assortment of plant species. During storms and landslips, these plants might end up getting washed into the sea individually or as mats of vegetation. The weevil larvae can survive for several days, protected by the tissues of their foodplants. This is better but is still not enough to explain how they traversed the distances between many of the islands. Another possibility is that weevil eggs deposited in fruits might be inadvertently consumed by fruit-eating birds and then deposited later on in its droppings. To test this tantalizing possibility, curious biologists did some experiments, poking the weevil eggs into fruit, feeding it to a range of bird species and then waiting to see what came out the other end. The eggs did indeed survive the rigours of the digestive tract of two thrush species and a bulbul, while those fed to a fruit-eating pigeon were digested. The long-range dispersal of these weevils in the gut of fruit-eating birds is a possibility then, but it is yet to be documented in the wild.

SHAPE

SPOONWING

Up until fairly recently, international travel was the preserve of the well-to-do, the dispossessed or the military. Very nearly 200 years ago, a couple of characters from the former camp, French painter and naturalist Jean Louis Florent Polydore Roux and the Austrian diplomat, botanist and explorer Charles von Hügel, were travelling through Egypt *en route* to Bombay. Writing about his time in Egypt, Roux is distinctly unimpressed by the lack of insects, but when poking about in the rock tombs around the great pyramids of Giza, probably looking for booty, he spots something amid the sand that does get him going, describing it thus: 'I encountered a small animal, so extraordinary, so singularly shaped … I take pleasure in sending you a drawing of it.' You can almost feel his excitement. He christened it *Necrophylus arenarius*, which translates as 'corpse-lover of the sand'.

What Roux found and beautifully drew was indeed singular. It was the larva of a spoonwing, which are among the most peculiar of all insect larvae. It looks like a guitar – the triangular head sporting a pair of sickle-like mandibles is attached to the soft, plump body via an impossibly long, thin neck. Adult spoonwings are no less dramatic, what with their extremely long, often ornate hind wings and mouthparts drawn into a long rostrum, which they use to feed on pollen. They are insects of semi-arid and arid lands across a good swathe of the planet, although at least half of the known 150 species are found only in South Africa. Even though they've been fluttering around for the best part of 150 million years, they're often scarce and the adults are rather short-lived.

The larvae of some species, like the one that Roux found, are specialists of small caves, rock overhangs and empty buildings. The larvae have stuck their neck out, literally, in pursuit of perfecting the art of ambush. Edging backwards into the sand, they remain concealed until prey blunders within range of their hypodermic jaws that inject venom and digestive enzymes. The long neck may also keep struggling prey away from the delicate body and allow the larvae to more safely find good sites to ambush from without falling prey to others of their kind. In other species, ones which lack the long neck, the larvae live deeper within the soil, opportunistically taking any prey that comes their way. This might not happen very often though. Larvae kept in captivity have been shown to survive for seven years without any food!

Spoonwings are not the strongest fliers, and their long, elegant hindwings may help them glide, but they're probably primarily a defence against predators, grabbing the attention of birds, which peck at these non-essential parts of the insect rather than the crucial bits. In some species, there are structures on the male's wing which might disseminate pheromones, although much of the biology of these unmistakable insects is still a mystery.

GIANT BLUE DUNG BEETLE

am in the Peruvian Amazon and the daylight is beginning to fade. Out of nowhere, a metallic blue, golf-ball-sized object flashes past me, the unmistakable buzz of insect wings the only clue to its identity.

This was my first encounter with the dung beetle *Coprophanaeus lancifer*, a truly stunning insect. The adults are on the wing for only a small window of each day, normally from about 4 pm until it gets dark. Their flight is incredibly rapid, purposeful and precise, navigating the tangled understorey of the sweltering forest. At a later date, I was able to watch them come to a foetid, baited trap and the precision of their flight as they hovered around the trap deciding whether or not to land was a delight to see.

They are among the largest dung beetles and up close they are truly something to behold. The body is compact and the male sports a prodigious horn on his head for sparring with other males. The broad bases of the limbs where they attach to the body are very wide, allowing for the attachment of some serious musculature. Grip one in your fist and it will push its way out, more normally using its remarkable strength to excavate deep tunnels and brood chambers.

Unlike nearly all of its relatives, this beetle has forsaken dung in favour of another food source – carrion. When any big animal across a great swathe of the Amazon Rainforest croaks, these big, beautiful beetles are among the first carrion specialists to arrive. Over what distance they can detect the early, heady odours of decay is unknown, but it must be several kilometres. When you see them zooming through the forest, they're on their way to a body. They have to be quick because carrion in these hot, humid environments doesn't last long and a huge cast of characters all want a piece of the action.

A large carcass will be enough for lots of beetles. On arrival, males and females will pair up and get stuck in, hacking off bits of the carcass using their heads like saws and excavating deep tunnels ending in brood chambers into which the chunks of meat will be dragged. The female lays her eggs in these brood chambers and her larvae consume the carrion.

With the exception of the carrion, all other dung beetles do the same sort of thing – stocking subterranean brood chambers with food for their offspring. Apart from a few other odd species that feed on millipedes or queen leafcutter ants, the food of choice is, unsurprisingly, dung. This preferred diet is what makes them so important ecologically – they're among the most efficient recyclers of animal waste. In agricultural systems where they have not been assaulted by insecticides, dung beetles provide vital services. Not only do they remove dung and suppress pests, but their tunnelling also improves soil structure and reduces surface run-off. They also feed lots of other animals and increase overall biodiversity. In the UK alone, it has been estimated that these services save the cattle industry some £367 million per year.

When you see them zooming through the forest, they're on their way to a body.

Far back into antiquity, dung beetles have been revered. The Sacred Scarab was very familiar to the Ancient Egyptians, who noted some of its life cycle and dung-rolling behaviour. These observations inspired elements of Egyptian mythology. To the Egyptians, the sun was reborn or created from nothing at the beginning of each day and rolled across the sky by an enormous dung beetle – their god Khepri. Khepri was the god of the rising or morning sun, creation and the renewal of life. The Egyptians saw only snippets of the beetle's life cycle. They witnessed them appear as if from nowhere and so assumed they had been created from nothingness, or, more disturbingly, that the male beetle could procreate by himself, simply by squirting his sperm into its ball of dung.

Dung beetles might not roll the sun across the sky, but they do keep their dung rolling to a straight course by using the position of the sun, the moon and even the Milky Way.

GIANT BLUE
DUNG BEETLE

These golf-ball-sized beetles hurtle through the rainforest, following the telltale odour that leads them to the carrion they feed on.

TWISTED-WING PARASITE

f you've ever felt sorry for mayflies and their famously short adult lives, please spare a thought for male Strepsipterans, who make mayflies seem positively venerable. In some species, the males live for barely a couple of hours. Even if they wanted to cling on for longer, they're doomed since they're bereft of functioning mouthparts and cannot feed.

In what little time they have, they must close the circle of one of the most remarkable life cycles of any insect. On their large, seemingly twisted wings, which give this group of insects their common name, they take to the air in a race against time to find a female. Fortunately, their large antler-like antennae are tuned into the pheromones wafted into the air from the female, a few molecules of which are enough to get the male twitching. The female can't simply waft her pheromones from a high perch and wait for the male to arrive. She is a parasite, living out her entire life in the body of a host, which could be a bee or wasp, although she parasitizes a great many insects. A passenger, the female goes where her host goes, complicating matters for her suitors who are racing against time.

Following the trail of pheromone molecules, the male manages to locate a female and with tenacious grip he clings on, piercing her head, the only part of her body that protrudes from the host, and injecting his sperm directly into her body cavity. This brutal means of reproduction is rightly known as traumatic insemination and is practised by a wide variety of insects, most famously bedbugs.

The remainder of the female's body takes up most of the host's abdomen, squeezing the sex organs to one side with some interesting consequences for the host; males can look like females and vice versa. Within the body of the sexually confused host, the female Strepsipteran's eggs, now fertilized, develop into tiny, very active larvae known as planidia, which move about in their mother's body cavity, using her like a swimming pool, until they eventually clamber out from the brood canal on her head.

These larvae have one job – they must latch onto a host, and they must do so quickly. Everything is against the clock with these insects and if the larvae can't find a host quickly, they'll exhaust their energy reserves and perish. In the species that depend on bees and wasps, the larvae might loiter on or near flowers, using the bristles at the end of their body to fling themselves into the air, hopefully latching onto a host and getting carried back to its nest. Once in the nest, the young Strepsipterans seek out and burrow into the bee/wasp larvae to develop as internal parasites. The hosts grow and will eventually pupate, although their internal organs are squeezed by the growing freeloaders. Only the male Strepsipterans, once adult, will leave theirs hosts, fluttering off to find host-bound females and close this bizarre life cycle.

Twisted by name, twisted by nature. To many, this account might feel rather gruesome, but to me it's astonishing and underscores just how rich and varied the lives of insects are.

LONG-TAILED DANCE FLY

n most animal species, reproduction requires a male and female and the gametes produced by their respective gonads. On the whole, males produce lots of small, biologically cheap gametes (sperm) which they want to scatter and dispense with abandon. In contrast, females produce fewer, large gametes (eggs) which require significantly more investment than sperm. This disparity is the basis for the wonderful, often perplexing variety of courtship rituals we see in animals and the generally testosterone-crazed behaviour of the males – from the courtship songs of the male Lesser Water Boatman, which it makes by scraping its penis across corrugations on its abdomen, to the incredible plumage of the male Peacock.

All of this is about wooing and impressing females. Females invest considerable resources in the production of their eggs, as well as nurturing them and even looking after the young, so it pays for them to be choosy, selecting the 'fittest' mate possible. The term *fit* is sometimes slang for 'attractive', but it also captures something of what biological 'fitness' is about.

In a relatively small number of species, these roles have been reversed and it is the females that have to woo the males. One of the most intriguing examples of this is in the Long-tailed Dance Fly. The females of this species cannot hunt for food, so they depend on prey – nuptial gifts – proffered by the males. This dependency means that the females have to impress the males. They do this by making their abdomen appear as large as possible – sucking in air to inflate it and then flattening it out, further accentuating their abdomen's width by holding their feathery legs against it. A larger abdomen can produce more eggs, and the potential to maximize reproductive potential is what the males are looking for.

The females of the fly compete with each other, flying around in tight formations called 'leks' which form about 10 minutes before sunrise and sunset and go on for about 40 minutes. There might be anywhere between 10 and 100 females in these leks. Males come flocking to check out the talent, flying through the small cloud of females several times until they decide on a mate. The females jockey for position in the lek, with the larger individuals hovering in the lower positions where the chances of being singled out by a male are greater.

Finally, when a male has made his selection, he flies up from below to within a centimetre or two of the female that attracts him. This is her signal, and she drops from the lek and the two of them zoom away from the swarm for their tryst. Of course, the female's starving. All that inflating of abdominal sacs and hovering has left her feeling more than a bit peckish and she's desperate to get her beak into the prey the male is holding – typically a small fly. He hands over the prey and the deal is sealed. Still on the wing, the pair mate and the ultimate objective of all of this posturing is achieved.

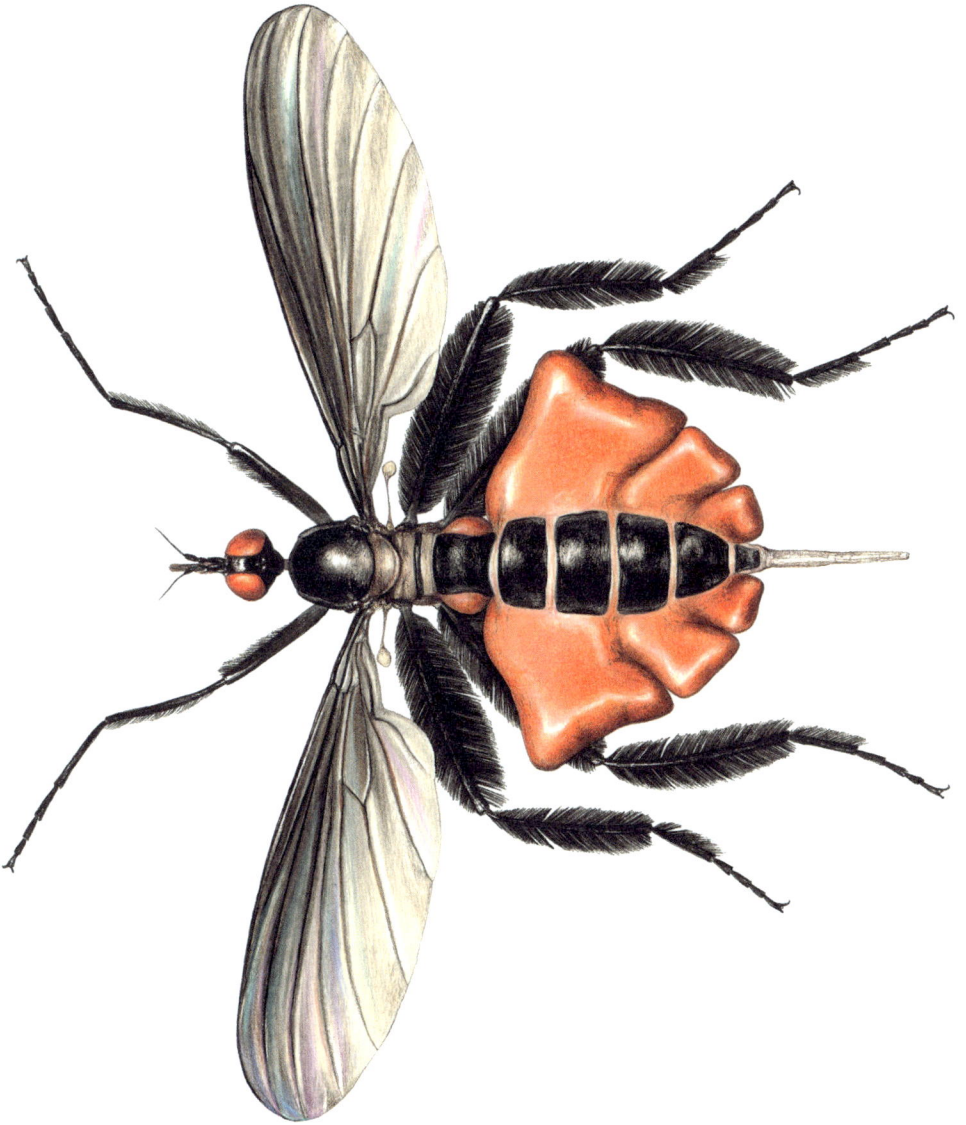

RHAMPHOMYIA LONGICAUDA ├───────────────────┤ EASTERN NORTH AMERICA

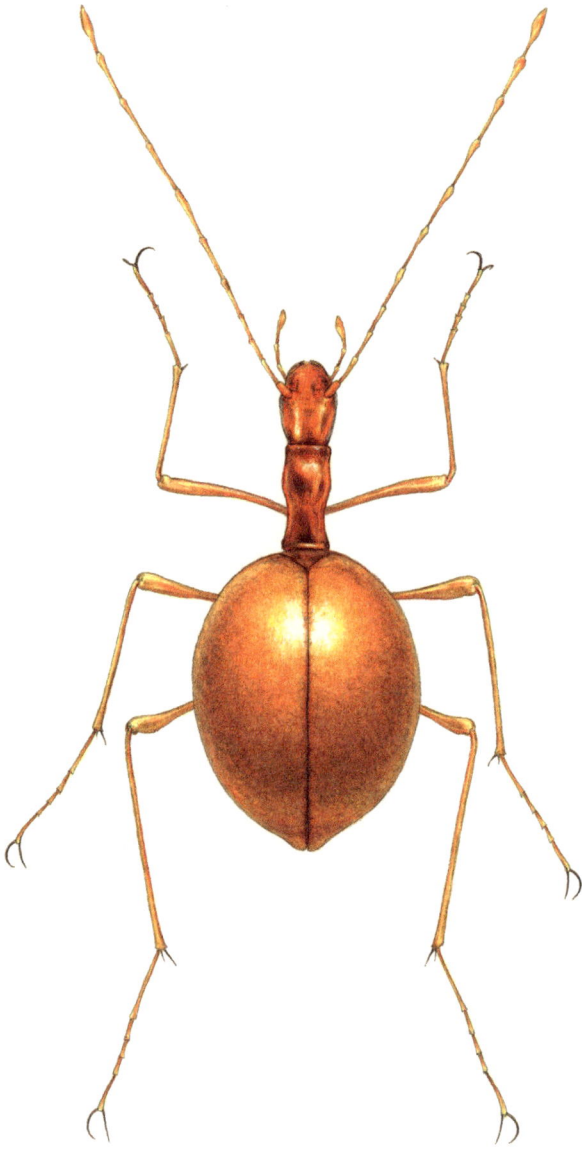

LEPTODIRUS HOCHENWARTII ├─────────────────┤

CAVE BEETLE

Evolution. Most people will have heard the term, even used it, but ask them to describe what it is, and they might struggle. The popular view is that evolution is a purposeful, one-way process where simple forms give rise to increasingly complex ones. As ever, the reality is much more interesting. Evolution has no purpose or direction and in adapting to a particular way of life an organism can progressively lose many, sometimes all, of its complex features. One place where we see some really fine examples of this is in caves.

The beetle shown here (*Leptodirus hochenwartii*), is an early troglobiont discovery, found when a cave guide called Luka Čeč, who was obviously a rather sharp-eyed and curious fellow, spotted one in 1831 in Slovenia. This insect is completely committed to a cave-dwelling existence, possessing a number of remarkable adaptations to a life in the cool air and pitch-blackness of the caves, a habitat where food is incredibly scarce. Its appendages are long and thin, a common trait among cave-dwelling insects and arachnids. These filamentous appendages allow it to feel its surroundings for any sign of edible morsels. It also lacks wings, pigment and eyes, all of which its above-ground ancestor would have had, but which were progressively lost as they shunned the light and became more and more adapted to a life deep underground. Pigment down there in the dark is of no use as there is no ultraviolet light to need protection from. Similarly, because they live in total darkness, eyes are of no use, so they've also dispensed with these. It might seem strange that an organ as complex as an eye can wither away over countless generations, but if it is surfeit to requirements this is exactly what happens. Ditto for wings and flight – not much use for underground and where calories to fuel big flight muscles are very thin on the ground.

The peculiar rotund elytra of this beetle are another interesting adaptation to this way of life. These form a dome which is used to store humid air that the beetle breathes, especially if it finds itself in slightly drier areas of the cave. These beetles also possess a special organ on their antennae which allows them to detect humidity levels, so they don't stray too far from their comfort zone when they search for food. When it comes to food, they can't afford to be picky. They nibble any organic matter they can find – bits of debris that have been washed into the cave, as well as bat and bird droppings. If they chance upon the carcass of a small animal, this would be cause for celebration – well, if they could celebrate and weren't so famished from not having enough to eat. Weirdly, this life of deprivation is probably a very long one. Exactly how long they live is unknown, but if other troglobionts are anything to tell by, it could be several years – much longer than any related species on the surface.

SEA SKATER

n the good old days of exploration, no expedition was complete without a naturalist, who often also doubled up as the doctor. This was the case with the Rurik expedition that set sail from St Petersburg in 1815, with the mission of discovering and exploring the Northwest Passage. During this expedition, the ship's doctor and naturalist Johann Friedrich von Eschscholtz collected lots of specimens and recorded his observations, among which were some curious, small insects he later named *Halobates*, now commonly called Sea Skaters because they are close relatives of Pond Skaters, those leggy animals we see gliding around on ponds, lakes and languid areas in rivers.

We now know of 40 Sea Skater species, found around the world in tropical and subtropical seas. Most of these species are coastal, although five of them are open-ocean species – often found hundreds of kilometres from the nearest land. This is extremely unusual for insects: out of more than one million species, only these five open-ocean Sea Skater species are exclusively marine, never coming to land.

Why are there no other marine insects? From an evolutionary point of view, insects are terrestrial crustaceans that descended from a marine animal which lived about 500 million years ago. The sea was a busy place, which drove these proto-insects to colonize and eventually conquer the land, freshwater and air. Today, the sea is still very busy, with few if any niches for insect-sized animals to exploit. Sea Skaters, living at the interface of air and sea, are as far as insects have got in returning to their roots.

To survive in what is a very extreme environment, Sea Skaters have evolved some singular adaptations. They're about as waterproof as you can get and spend a great deal of their life 'grooming' themselves, using their spindly legs to smear waxy secretions over their body. These secretions coat a layer of tiny, dense mushroom-shaped hairs that cover their body. With these wax-covered hairs, the Sea Skaters are effectively non-wettable. The hairs also trap a layer of air that make them super buoyant and allow them to breathe underwater if they're inadvertently submerged by rough seas or predator attacks. You won't be surprised to learn that engineers are studying the structure of these hairs and the composition of the secretions to make water-repellent and low-friction coatings.

Being small, flightless and restricted to the surface of the sea, Sea Skaters are exposed to an amount of UV and infrared rays that would frazzle any other animal. Some property of their exoskeleton or the waxy secretions, the nature of which is unknown, shield them from these damaging rays – yet more things for engineers interested in biomimetics to explore.

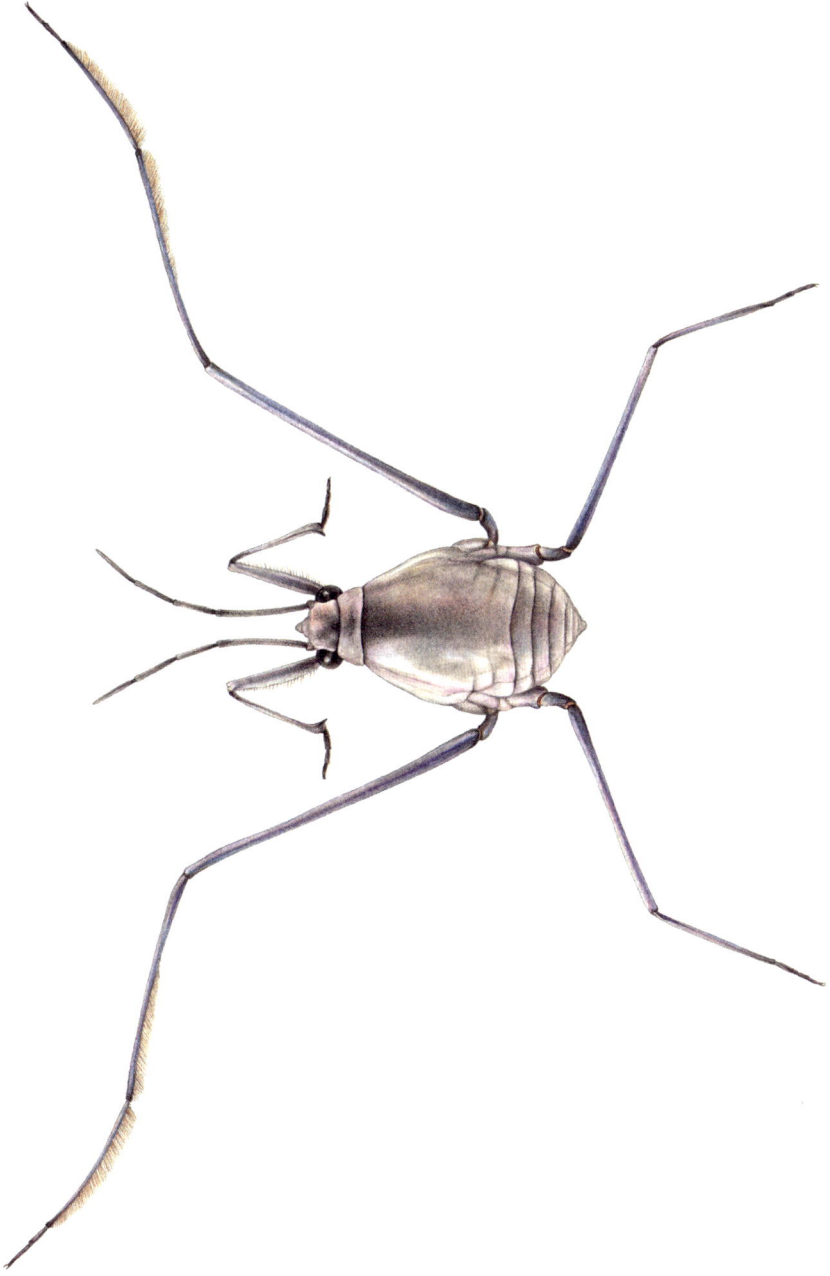

MOON MOTH

I f moths were capable of being affronted, I'm pretty sure they would be quivering with rage at always being dismissed as dowdy, creepy versions of butterflies. Not only are there lots of colourful moths, but they are also way more diverse than butterflies. Actually, this competition is meaningless anyway because butterflies are moths – they're effectively just day-flying moths that first took to this way of life about 98 million years ago.

Moon Moths are a perfect example of how beautiful these animals can be, with large wings tapering into long 'tails' that look like they're simply for the sake of style. It turns out the real reason for these elegant wings is much more interesting.

Most moths are nocturnal, which is good news if you're not keen on them and even better news for bats, their main predators. Bats evolved a long time after moths and it may be that this nocturnal banquet of winged protein was an alluring carrot to the scampering, insectivorous and tree-dwelling mammal that would go on to give rise to bats.

The urge to eat and to not get eaten has set up some remarkable evolutionary arms races, none more so than between moths and bats. For one thing, pursuing the items on the aerial buffet led to the evolution of flight in bats, the only group of mammals where this has ever happened. To fly at night and to pinpoint fast-moving prey also requires some pretty sharp senses and bats ticked that box by evolving echolocation – effectively 'seeing' with sound rather than light.

In turn, moths have had to adapt to these threats, evolving countermeasures to keep one step ahead of these new and terrifying predators. Moths were equipped with ears before bats came on the scene, but as these predators evolved and honed the ability to see with sound, moths needed to be able to tune in to these distinctive, high-pitch frequencies, especially the ones which indicated when a bat was zeroing in. Moths can do this, allowing them to make evasive manoeuvres, such as dropping out of the sky or taking cover in foliage just before the bat strikes. Some moths have even evolved the ability to produce their own high-frequency sounds to advertise their toxicity to hungry bats. Remarkably, the sounds produced by some moths can even 'jam' the echolocation calls of bats, confusing them and giving the moth a chance to escape. There are even moths that shed fluffy material into the air which reflect the hunting clicks of a bat, creating a cloud of false targets. This is the same principle as the chaff dispensed by aircraft to disrupt radar. You can now see why the terms 'evolutionary arms race' is rather apt.

The urge to eat and to not get eaten has set up some remarkable evolutionary arms races …

In the case of the Moon Moths, the long tails of the wings reflect the sound in a way that dupes the bat and instead of lunging for the front part of the moth, where all of the really important bits are, the bat goes for the tails, which are flimsy and break off. The moth flutters off into the night, more or less unscathed, and the bat is left confused and hungry. Not only that, but the scales covering the wings of some moths also absorb the bat's echolocating clicks, giving them a cloak of invisibility. Understanding the structure of these scales may give us new sound-absorbing materials that have all sorts of applications in the modern world.

MOON MOTH

The elegant tails of these moths serve as decoy, reflecting the hunting calls of bats and attracting attention away from the moth's body.

MOLE CRICKET

As humans, vision is our primary sense, so our appreciation and understanding of the natural world is dominated by the information we receive through our eyes. Beyond form, colour and texture there are soundscapes and 'aromascapes', of which we can perceive only snippets – the full extent is beyond the range of our more obviously limited hearing and smell.

For us, birdsong is the most conspicuous element of nature's soundscape, but there is a whole cast of other, smaller performers creating a true symphony of sound beyond the range of our hearing, from the penis stridulations of the Lesser Water Boatman to the buzzing courtship songs of male spiders. There are other performers who do sing within the range of human hearing, but they are seldom seen. One such animal is the Mole Cricket.

These insects are exquisitely adapted to an underground way of life, using their powerful, heavily modified forelimbs to dig surprisingly quickly, excavating burrows that vary depending on their purpose. The most remarkable of these is the burrow constructed by the male to amplify and resonate his courtship song. This particular burrow is, effectively, a Y-shaped horn with two openings at the surface. The male sits a few centimetres underground with his rear end directed at the confluence of these two branches, rubbing the edges of his forewings together to produce his distinctive, pure-tone, stridulatory chirp. With the resonance provided by the burrow, the volume of the song as it escapes into the air is 115 decibels and the tone is powerful enough to vibrate the ground all around the burrow up to a distance of 20 cm. When you consider the size of the animal – a mere 3–5 cm – this is quite some sound system.

During the breeding season, female Mole Crickets take to the wing at night to listen to these songs, the ears on their front legs pricked at a range of about 30 m. It is the volume of the song that really gets them going, as it's indicative of a larger male in good-quality habitat. The loudest males might have females queuing up outside their burrow, attracting 20 of them a night. Smaller quieter males will sing in vain, unable to attract any attention at all.

LONG-PROBOSCID FLY

Nearly every human culture has a thing for flowers, using them liberally in celebrations and commiserations. Yet flowers aren't really meant for us. Rather, they're complex, immersive adverts directed mostly at insects, which broadcast the availability of sugary water – nectar. There's always a catch, however, and to get at the nectar the insects must inadvertently pick up or get dusted with pollen.

The relationship between flowering plants and insects is one of the most significant in the history of life on Earth, completely transforming terrestrial ecosystems. In part, the colossal diversity of insects and plants are a direct result of this relationship, a symbiosis that is at least 160 million years old. It began with ancient insects getting dusted with pollen on one plant that was normally wind-pollinated and moving it to another plant of the same species. Natural selection got to work on these nascent beginnings and the interaction became increasingly sophisticated, with the evolution of dedicated structures designed to offer enticements and deliver just the right amount of pollen: flowers.

Fast-forward to the present day and the success of this strategy is hard to miss: the majority of flowering plant species are pollinated by insects, not to mention 75% of our crop species. This makes insect pollination crucial to life on land and our own survival.

This strategy is wildly successful and often used to illustrate how lovely and harmonious nature is, but the charming image of a bee at a flower belies a complex struggle. In return for carrying some of its pollen, the plant seeks to give the insect the minimum wage in nectar, while the insect wants maximum reward for minimum effort. This conflict has led to extreme specialization in flowers and pollinators, which is beautifully demonstrated in the fynbos of southern Africa, where a collection of Long-proboscid Fly species pollinate well over 200 plant species.

As their name suggests, these flies have exceptionally long mouthparts, which they've evolved to reach the nectar in the long, tubular flowers of their host plants, picking up a small amount of pollen in the process. The most extreme and well known of these species, *Moegistorhynchus longirostris*, sports a proboscis that can be just over 80 mm long – the longest mouthparts, in relation to body size, of any insect. When not in use, this ludicrously long structure is hinged backwards, tucked between the fly's legs.

The flies and the plants are locked into an unbreakable contract that highlights the fragility of ecosystems. The flies' mouthparts are too long and unwieldy to suckle nectar from any other flowers, while the flower's long, tubular nectary precludes less well-equipped pollinators.

MOEGISTORHYNCHUS LONGIROSTRIS ├─────────────┤ SOUTH AFRICA

GIANT BAMBOO WEEVIL

'I am joined with no foot land-rakers, no long-staff sixpenny strikers, none of these mad mustachio purple-hued malt-worms; but with nobility and tranquillity …' Shakespeare was a purveyor of put-downs, a connoisseur of contumely language, but this one, from *Henry IV*, is particularly interesting to me because the barbed Bard is dipping his quill in the world of entomology. In his time, 'malt-worms' was the name given to the grubs of the Grain Weevil, a pest species that can quickly run amok through stores of barley, wheat, oats, rye, rice and corn. The word was also used as an insult, directed at persons who quaffed too much booze.

The depredations of the Grain Weevil through human history have, by association, not done all that many favours for this group of insects, which is unfortunate given how astonishingly diverse they are. Along with the rove beetles, the weevils are the largest family of animals on the planet, with approximately 77,000 species worldwide. With the exception of the inhospitable climes of Antarctica, weevils are found just about everywhere. The vast majority of them are plant feeders, which is one reason why we live in such a weevily world. The blooming of plants back in the Mesozoic led to an explosion in their diversity, which, in turn, was mirrored by their attendant herbivores, including the weevils.

Weevil diversity exploded to exploit the new niches that were opening up. Today, there's a weevil for every part of a plant, from the roots to the seeds and everything in between. In adapting to specific niches, some weevils have forsaken plants in favour of flesh. These big, handsome weevils from South America are one such species. In 1928, the Portuguese agriculturalist Edmundo Navarro de Andrade revealed a remarkable nugget on the biology of these beetles when he was opening up segments of bamboo to see what the beetles were getting up to, since their activities could damage commercially important species of these giant grasses.

He found the weevil larvae were numerous when small, with six to ten in each bamboo internode, but at a later stage there was only one large fat larva present. Where had the other larvae gone in these later-stage nurseries? After opening up lots of weevily internodes, he finally found his answer and watched with great interest as a large larva ate one of its smaller siblings. *Rhinastus* weevils are cannibalistic.

With more time and observations – the currency of all good discoveries – the curious Navarro de Andrade found that the young larvae nibble the lining of their bamboo internode, or segment, but then for reasons that are still unclear, one of the larvae develops a taste for flesh and starts tucking into its brothers and sisters, until it dwells alone in the internode, plump and ready to pupate. Following pupation, the adult chews an exit hole to escape from the bamboo, before leading a rather fleeting life of only seven to eight days.

SAW-NOSED LANTERNFLY

This spectacular insect, with an extraordinary spiky process issuing from its head (the function of which is still unknown), has nothing to do with lanterns or flies. It is actually a true bug, in the same order of insects as aphids and shield bugs. Lanternflies are among the largest true bugs – up to 95 mm in some species – and all of them are sap suckers, using their straw-like mouthparts to pierce plants in order to suck up the sugary juices within. Sap is mostly water, so to extract enough nutrients any sap-feeder must imbibe huge quantities. To avoid bloating and exploding, these insects have an extremely efficient means of getting rid of the excess fluid quickly, which they excrete as honeydew. This mildly sugary fluid is coveted by all sorts of other insects – there are even some moths and snails that wait eagerly at the rear end of lanternflies to lap greedily at the honeydew as it squirts out.

In addition to their sap-sucking abilities, lanternflies are prodigious jumpers, employing a combination of muscle power and the extraordinary elastic properties of a protein called resilin. This elastic protein is found in many parts of the body, from limbs to wing hinges and mouthparts. It can store about 92% of the energy loaded into it when stretched or squeezed. For comparison, the best synthetic rubbers can store about 80%. In lanternflies, large muscles ratchet back structures above the insect's legs, storing the energy in the resilin and allowing it to be released with explosive force when the insect wants to leap. In smaller relatives of lantern-flies, gears at the topmost hind-leg joints keep the legs perfectly together to channel the explosive force from the resilin into a straight jump.

Jumping is but one superpower of lanternflies and just one of the ways they evade their many enemies. Often, their first line of defence, before resorting to jumping and flying, is revealing their hindwings, which tend to be brightly coloured or adorned with large eyespots. This behaviour serves to startle large predators, who assume the 'eyes' belong to another large animal that can't easily be overpowered. One final neat trick lanternflies have is to produce waxy secretions. Depending on the species, these can be produced in long filaments and plumes from the back end of the insect.

This waxy material has a number of functions. Not only does it direct the atten-tion of bird and mammal predators away from the insect's head, but it also gives it a degree of protection from parasitoid wasps. The eggs of the lanternflies and their relatives are extremely vulnerable to egg parasitoids and a coating of thick, fluffy wax gives them a degree of defence against these enemies.

CATHEDRA SERRATA ├────────────────────┤ TROPICAL SOUTH AMERICA

ALLOMANTISPA MIRIMACULATA ├────────────────────┤ MYANMAR & CHINA

MANTISFLY

've been lucky enough to visit the fabled Htamanthi Wildlife Sanctuary, a 2,150 km² forest in the north of Myanmar. Home to tigers and elephants, this reserve also once supported Javan and Sumatran rhinoceros. It is difficult to get to and, apart from perhaps some general butterfly collecting when the country was under British colonial rule, I doubt that any entomologists have visited.

During my time in the reserve, a small team of us were away from base camp on the trail of tigers and I was catching any interesting insects we came across. Along the way, we were distracted by Western Hoolock Gibbons, an endangered ape, and we decided to try to get some footage of them. To do this required a strange game of musical statues to get as close as possible to the apes: running through the undergrowth during their raucous songs and pausing stock-still when they fell silent. During one of these pauses, an insect fluttered into my face and I promptly grabbed it. I was delighted to see it was a fairly large mantisfly and an unusual one at that. I carefully got it into a container and eventually into the Natural History Museum in London. The museum confirmed it was unusual – there was nothing else like it in the collection and it was later described as a new genus and species, *Allomantispa mirimaculata*.

These are fascinating insects on many levels. Superficially, they look a bit like praying mantises, but this is just a classic case of convergent evolution, where two completely unrelated species end up resembling one another because they have similar lifestyles. Mantisflies are closely related to lacewings and antlions. As adults they're ambush predators, sitting still on a leaf or branch and waiting for unsuspecting prey to come within range of their raptorial front legs that are armed with cruel spines.

As larvae, their lives are even more secretive and poorly known. Some species are predators of small arthropods, while others are parasitoids of bee, wasp or Scarab Beetle larvae. The most remarkable mantisfly larvae are those that are specialist parasitoids of spiders. In these species, the female mantisfly may deposit a clutch of eggs near the web of a spider heavy with eggs or, more adventurously, cling to the spider's abdomen until she constructs an egg sac. The mantisfly larvae, when they hatch, might make straight for the egg sac if it's available, or they kill time in the spider's book lungs. Once the mantisfly larvae are successfully inside the egg sac, they go to town, enjoying the eggs as though they were coconuts – slurping up the contents via a feeding tube.

The larval biology of the genus I discovered in Myanmar is unknown. They're typically very rare. Perhaps they spend most of their time in the canopy. Perhaps their biology is even more remarkable than the spider-egg slurpers and even more of a lottery, where the chances of any one larva reaching adulthood are very, very small.

ANT-NEST HOVERFLY

A
s adults, hoverflies are delicate animals of the air. Perhaps the most accomplished flying animals there have ever been, they fly at speed, some species migrating huge distances as well as hovering with extreme precision, darting in any direction between nectar sources. In the warmer months, it's always well worth spending some time watching these insects to appreciate their phenomenal ability in the air.

In stark contrast to the delicate, nectar- and sap-sipping adults, the larvae of many species are predators, dispatching a whole range of prey. Among the most bizarre of these are the larvae of *Microdon* hoverflies – strange, domed animals that look like miniature tanks and reside only within ant nests. Their appearance is so strange that they were initially thought to be molluscs or scale insects.

Ant nests might be well defended, but they offer a stable climate and a smorgasbord of food, from plump larvae and pupae to the rich pickings of refuse heaps, all of which has attracted a great many unsavoury characters, including the likes of *Microdon*. Trundling around the dark confines of the nest, they plunder the ant's brood. The mature larvae of one *Microdon* species have been observed consuming as many as 10 ant larvae in a 30-minute period, which indicates quite some appetite. The fly larva clambers on top of the helpless ant larva, pierces it with its mouthparts and sucks it dry. Sometimes, attendant worker ants come along and drag their young sister away from the marauder. Normally though, the ants just leave the *Microdon* larvae to it, even picking up the discarded husk of one of their sisters and carrying it to the refuse pile. What the younger *Microdon* larvae eat is unknown, but it has been suggested they might consume the droplets of liquid food produced by the ant larvae, which is what adult worker ants do.

If another insect was to attempt this – a chancer, say, from outside – it would swiftly get torn to pieces. Living off ants, within their nests, is not for opportunists; rather, it requires some serious specialization. Firstly, the domed body of the *Microdon* larva is some protection from the ants if things do happen to turn nasty. Its primary defence, though, is a chemical cloak – the odours it produces from its body are exactly the same as the host ant. Odours are at the heart of ant communication and the way the whole colony operates. Tap into this channel by mimicking the odour of the ants and you're on to a winner, free to wander the galleries, tunnels and chambers of the nest with impunity, more or less.

When the *Microdon* larva has had its fill of ant larva, it prepares to pupate, exuding a small droplet of clear brown fluid that is extremely attractive to the host ants, the purpose of which is unknown. When it emerges, the adult fly lacks the defences of its larval form, so it must swiftly make for the exit to avoid being attacked by the ants that it parasitized.

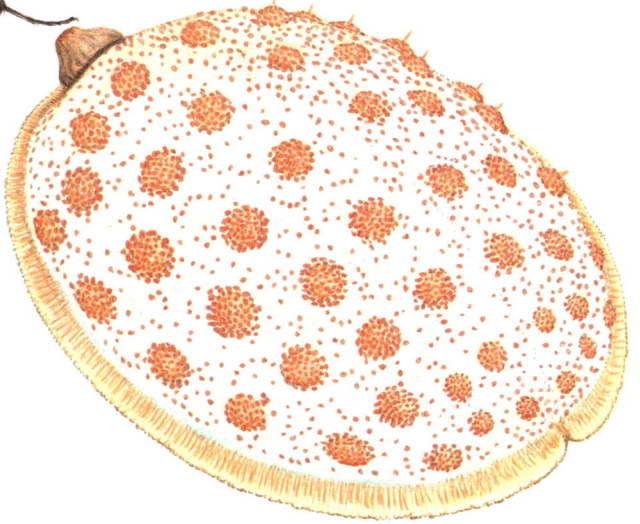

SABRE WASP

There's so much more to wasps than most people realize. For one thing, they are enormously diverse. Beetles are vaunted as the most diverse group of insects, but that perhaps has more to do with their popularity among collectors. In reality, wasps are probably as diverse as beetles, if not more so. Then there are the flies, but let's not get into that here. Most wasps – and certainly the ones that are least known – are tiny parasitoids (see Fairy Wasp – page 82), but plenty of them are substantial and much more difficult to miss. Cue the Sabre Wasp.

What looks like a tail protruding from the back end of this animal is actually a complex, multifunctional organ – the ovipositor. Principally for the laying of eggs, the ovipositor has also been co-opted as a syringe for the injection of a chemical cocktail we know as venom. In the Sabre Wasp, this structure has a third function as a drill bit, since the quarry of these wasps – various wood-munching insect larvae – live deep inside tree trunks.

The detection of these larvae is no mean feat; they are hidden out of sight and protected by several centimetres of wood. The wasp must draw on its incredibly sharp senses, especially its nose. I say 'nose', but I don't mean a pointy thing on its face, which is a mammalian trait. The sense of smell, regardless of where the 'nose' is or what it looks like, is all about detecting chemicals, and insects have 'noses' on their antennae and on the short appendages called palps near their mouthparts. The female wasp homes in on the telltale plume of odours emanating from the unaware host larvae. Alighting on the tree trunk, the wasp taps its antennae on the bark, trying to pinpoint the best place to drill. The ovipositor, or sting, or drill, is now brought into play, the wasp arching its body and standing on tiptoes to accommodate its length.

The tube of the ovipositor is a stunning work of nature ...

The tube of the ovipositor is a stunning work of nature, and actually composed of three separate elements, each of which can slide past each other a little way. Through a complex arrangement of muscles and other linkages, the reciprocal sliding of these elements moves the ovipositor through the wood towards its target. Not only that, but the tip of each of the ovipositor elements is hardened with manganese and equipped with sensory organs, allowing the wasp to cut through the wood with greater ease and to 'feel' its way.

Eventually, the tunnel of the host larva is breached, and the wasp feels for the unfortunate occupant using its sensitive ovipositor, which now reveals its other functions. Firstly, it stings the host, injecting venom to cause a rapid, but temporary paralysis, which prevents the victim from thrashing about and damaging the wasp's delicate bits. Next, the egg has to be squeezed down the entirety of the long, thin ovipositor, so to make this easier the egg is sausage-shaped. The egg is deposited on or very near the host, where it will hatch and then cling on tenaciously. At this point it waits for the host to grow as big as possible and for it to tunnel its way to very near the surface in preparation for its own pupation – a pupation that will never come. Sensing the hormones in the host's body which signal this change, the quiescent wasp larva now springs into action and consumes its dinner in short order.

The long egg-laying tube of this wasp doubles up as a drill bit for reaching the wood-boring insect larvae that are its prey.

BISON WASP

Even by insect standards, Bison Wasps are outlandish, preposterous even – a perfect example of why there can be no creator. To come up with these, the creator would have had to have been out of their mind on horse tranquilizers. Through the lens of natural selection, though, what appears outlandish in our eyes makes much more sense.

These wasps – about 25 known species, with many more still to discover – are mainly from the Neotropics where they are parasitoids of ants. Beyond their overall shape, from their relatively enormous thorax to the delicate stalked abdomen, perhaps their oddest characteristic is the horns that sprout from their thorax. Without any knowledge of the biology of these animals, you might say that these horns look like a bit of an impediment, but they do have an important function. They are actually tiny handles used by the host ants to carry the adult wasp from the nests when it emerges after developing in the nest within one of the ant larva.

To get inside the nest in the first place is a tortuous process, beset with all manner of pitfalls. The worker ants are on high alert for anything that doesn't belong in their nest, so these wasps have evolved a complex way of avoiding detection. They deposit their eggs on plants near the nest and the tiny, active larvae that hatch have to surreptitiously hitch a ride on a worker ant or potential prey that the ants are likely to catch and bring back to the nest.

If this goes according to plan and the wasp larva manages to get through undetected, the next hurdle is to get to a mature ant larva. It may achieve this by clambering between workers, eventually hopping onto a mature larva when it's being fed by one of the worker ants. Its mission nearly complete, the wasp larva now attaches to the ant larva and waits for it to pupate. When this happens, the young wasp burrows into the host and consumes it. All has gone to plan so far, but there's still the thorny issue of the adult wasp getting out of the ant nest alive.

When it emerges as an adult, the adult wasp mimics the odour of the ant's nest, but not perfectly. Mistaking the wasp for a bit of detritus that needs to be removed from the nest, a worker ant grabs it by its handles and carries it to the exit where the wasp flies off to find a mate. Finding one another is a real challenge for small animals, so the male Bison Wasps have elaborate, antler-like antennae for detecting the merest whiffs – individual molecules of female pheromones that can be followed like a trail of breadcrumbs to their source, closing the loop on this extraordinary life cycle.

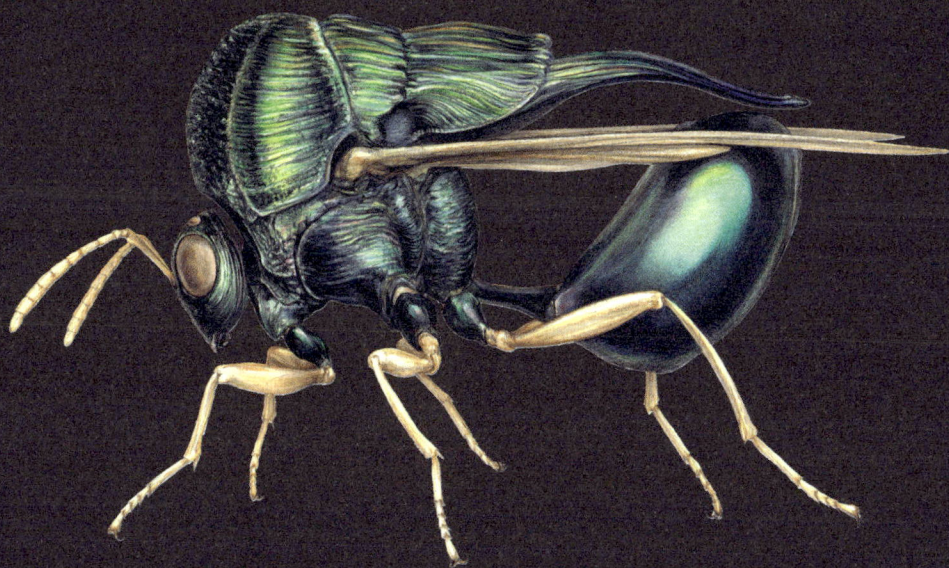

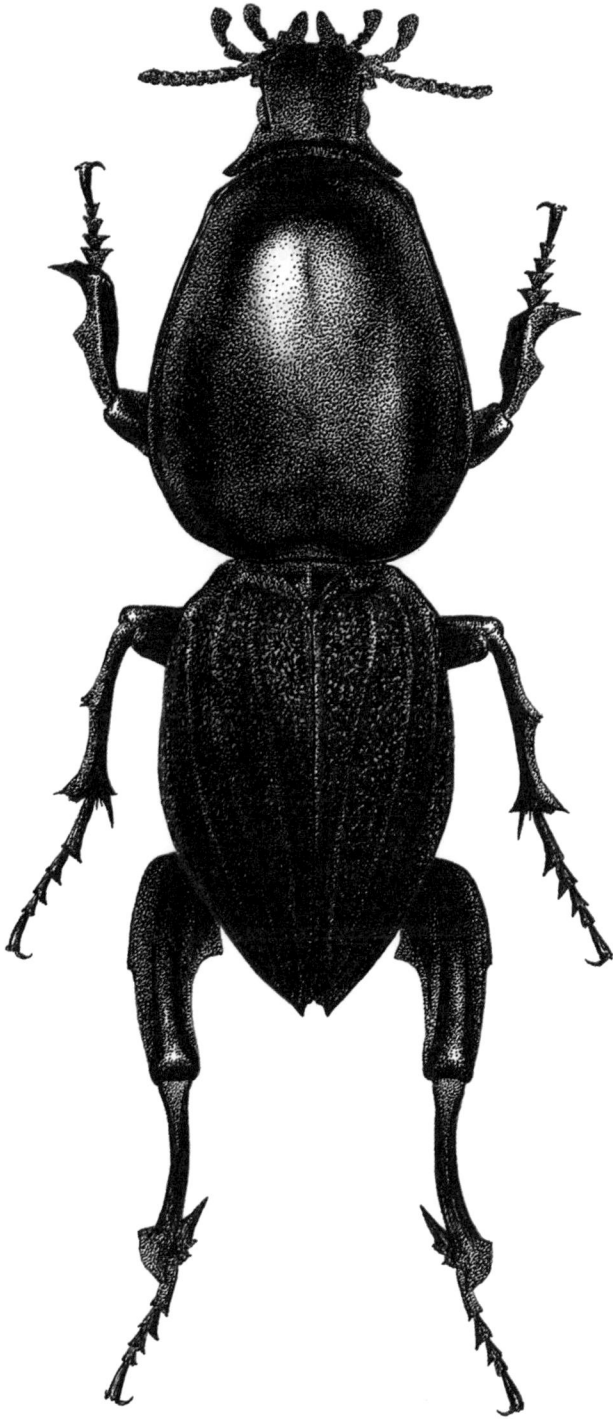

MOLE BEETLE

Within every group of animals, there are species that have caused a great deal of head-scratching among the people who study them. The Mole Beetle is the insect equivalent of the platypus; its combination of features makes it very difficult to classify.

We now know it is actually a type of Longhorn Beetle that, in adapting to a subterranean way of life, has come to look very much like a Mole Cricket (see page 163), demonstrating the power of evolutionary convergence to mould similar forms from very different starting points. This is perhaps one of the finest examples of convergent evolution there is.

For the most part, Longhorn Beetles live on or in plants, and the adults, fairly conspicuous and often large, are among the most sought-after insects by collectors. There are some that, as larvae, have taken to life underground, where they nibble plant roots.

Normally reaching about 5 cm long, but sometimes as much as 7 cm, Mole Beetles are only known to inhabit a small part of eastern Brazil in the states of Minas Gerais and Bahia. Next to nothing is known about their biology because they spend most of their life underground. You can see footage of them online, male specimens scurrying awkwardly across dirt roads, their limbs and bodies poorly adapted for walking on the surface. In becoming burrowing animals, the elytra have fused and the wings have long since been dispensed. Walking is their only way of getting about, hence their very limited range. Exactly how the male uses his extremely well-developed hind legs has never been documented, but it is very likely they're used in courtship, perhaps for fighting other males.

It is thought these wandering males, probably recently emerged as adults, are seeking out females, typically at the beginning of the rainy season in December and January. More rotund than the males and with less developed legs, the females appear to spend their entire life underground, so even less is known about them.

BEE FLY

n many temperate locations, Bee Flies (*Bombyliidae*) are auguries of spring, among the first insects to put in an appearance after the long drudgery of winter. I always find it heartening to see these fluffy little characters, but then I remember how they live and what they do to solitary bees. Their charming appearance belies a parasitic way of life.

The furry pelage of these flies insulates them from the vagaries of the spring weather. In the sunshine, you will see them basking on the ground, poking their rigid proboscis into flowers to sip nectar, and hovering intently above the nests of their hosts – ground-nesting solitary bees.

The female Bee Fly, in preparation for the final act of her short adult life, seeks out a patch of dry soil or sand and grinds the tip of her abdomen against it, filling a small pouch with particles of the material. She then takes off to seek out the nests of her hosts. Hovering expertly above these nests, identifying them by visual and perhaps chemical cues, she coats each egg in a ballast of sand and flicks them towards the dark, inviting openings of the nest entrances. Egg production can be impressive, up to 3,000 eggs per day in some species, a consequence of a very high-stakes lifestyle since only a tiny proportion of the eggs will make it through successfully to adulthood.

Active, mobile larvae, which are called planidia, hatch quickly and make for the nest hole if their mother's aim was off. Once inside the nest, odours direct the active larvae towards the brood chambers of the host where, if they're lucky, they'll feed, grow and metamorphose twice – a type of development known as hypermetamorphosis. In the first metamorphosis, the active larva, after perhaps scoffing some of the stored pollen in the brood chamber, transforms into a more typical grub. Then, things take a slightly darker turn. Tired of eating pollen, the newly transformed Bee Fly larva turns its attention to the original inhabitant of the brood chamber, the solitary bee larva. It consumes the helpless bee larva in its entirety, growing sufficiently to metamorphose a second time, this time into the adult.

At any point along this long journey from egg to adult, things can go wrong for the Bee Fly. The aim of the female might be woefully inaccurate, and the larva may hatch too far from the host nest, drying to a husk before it gets inside. Near or in the nest, the solitary bee might discover the Bee Fly larva and kill it. In the brood chamber, microbes might destroy the food stores and both larvae. Even if the Bee Fly larva negotiates all of these pitfalls and successfully pupates, it has to sit out the winter, when it is at the mercy of wet conditions and mould. Given all of these challenges, it is remarkable that any of them make it, but they do.

WIDE-EYED FUNGUS WEEVIL

Sexual reproduction is one of the key innovations in the story of life on Earth. It allows the genetic deck to be shuffled, providing the variation that natural selection can get to work on. It is also a curse – the genders locked into a ceaseless struggle to get their genes into the next generation. This struggle is at its most obvious in male animals, who vie with each other to woo females, spending time, energy and resources on behaviours and all sorts of adornments, from Botox to the impressive mouthparts of stag beetles. In many cases, the courtship contests between males never actually break into real scuffles because these can end in mortal injuries. Instead, the males will simply size each other up based on their adornments, and a weedy male will think twice before taking on a more physically impressive opponent.

In some insects, the selection pressure to size each other up has led to the evolution of some unusual traits. Among the most curious of these is a massive, lateral expansion of the head, which reaches its zenith in the well-known Stalk-eyed Flies – the eyes of which are at the end of long stalks. Less known, but along the same lines, are the Wide-eyed Fungus Weevils (*Exechesops leucopsis*), the males of which sport massively enlarged, flared heads, the eyes widely separated.

In these weevils, receptive females who are eager to mate attract males by clambering to a conspicuous spot on the host snowbell tree and doing a song and dance routine. By scraping her abdomen against the inner face of her elytra, she produces a rasping song, accompanied by her dance – quickstep rotations to the left and right, perhaps to broadcast her song over the greatest area possible.

The little males – they're just under 1 cm long – come flocking, establishing territories in prime spots on the snowbell fruit. It is here that the super-wide heads of the males come into play, used now as a weapon to exclude other males from their territory. The males will shove each other using their heads like battering rams, but this happens only if the males are very equally matched. Normally, sizing each other up based on eye width is enough; males facing off with obviously larger opponents will readily flee, long before there's any argy-bargy.

Large males with the widest faces are more likely to successfully defend a territory, which is what the females are looking for. After mating, to give his sperm the best chance of fertilizing the female's eggs, the male will stand guard, squaring up to other males who fancy a go. As with some other insects, it's possible there are less impressive males that opt for a sneakier approach to mating, surreptitiously copulating with a receptive female while the larger males jostle over who has the widest face.

FURTHER READING

Bert Hölldobler and Christina L Kwapich, *The Guests of Ants: How Myrmecophiles Interact with Their Hosts*, Belknap Press, 2022

Eric R Eaton, *Wasps: The Astonishing Diversity of a Misunderstood Insect*, Princeton University Press, 2021

Jean-Henri Fabre, *Fabre's Book of Insects*, Tudor Publishing Company, 1921
  A classic book of natural history observation.

Maxwell V L Barclay and Patrice Bouchard, *Beetles of the World: A Natural History (A Guide to Every Family)*, Princeton University Press, 2023

Scott Richard Shaw, *Planet of the Bugs – Evolution and the Rise of Insects*, University of Chicago Press, 2014
  A superb overview of where insects came from and what makes them so successful.

Simon van Noort and Gavin R Broad, *Wasps of the World: A Guide to Every Family*, Princeton University Press, 2024

Stephen A Marshall, *Flies: The Natural History and Diversity of Diptera*, Firefly Books Ltd, 2012

Stephen A Marshall, *Beetles: The Natural History and Diversity of Coleoptera*, Firefly Books Ltd, 2018

Stephen A Marshall, *Hymenoptera: The Natural History and Diversity of Wasps, Bees and Ants*, Firefly Books Ltd, 2023

ABOUT THE AUTHOR

Entomologist and zoologist Dr Ross Piper has been fascinated by insects for as long he can remember. Always eager to scrabble around in the undergrowth and root around in rotting logs, his work has taken him around the world and resulted in a new genus and several new species. To share his enthusiasm for the natural world, Piper has presented at various international events, written numerous books and articles, and contributed to TV programmes for the BBC and the Smithsonian Institution, both as an on-screen expert and a consultant. For more info see rosspiper.net.

ABOUT THE ILLUSTRATOR

Carim Nahaboo is a natural history artist who specializes in entomological illustration. His works are traditionally hand drawn usings ink, coloured pencil and, at times, acrylic. In addition to drawing his subjects, from an early age Nahaboo has looked for British insects and reared various exotic species, learning firsthand about their behaviour and anatomy. This scientific fascination has always gone hand in hand with the drive to explore and understand entomology through art, in order to capture some of the wonder and beauty of the insect world.

INDEX

ACKNOWLEDGEMENTS

I am indebted to the talented people who have helped bring this book into being. Tina Persaud first approached me with the idea and was instrumental in the early stages of the project. Philip Contos at Laurence King steered it through the waters of publication. Katherine Pitt and Kate Shanahan both lent their editorial expertise to the project, using their astute eyes to help refine the content. Designer Hannah Owens has a fine aesthetic sense and has created what I think is an exquisite book. Both she and I were fortunate to have Carim Nahaboo illustrating the content. The quality of his work is second to none. Not only that, but he has a deep interest in these animals, which made the commissioning of the works a pleasure. We discussed the shortlist of species, and without prompt, he knew the best way to illustrate each of them. I urge you to take a look at Carim's online presence, as many of his works can be purchased as prints. Thanks also to Tony Wigmore and Ken Prew for discussions on the species included in the book, and for help finding some of them in the field. Finally, I should probably thank my family for allowing me to subject them to more insect chat than usual while working on this book.

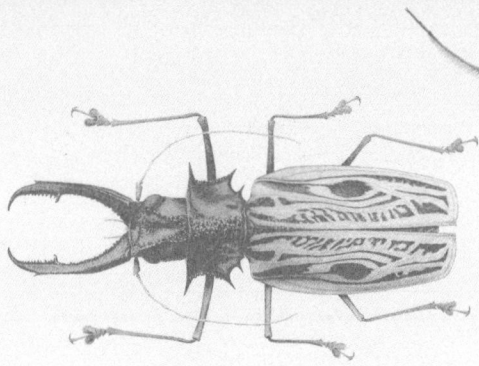

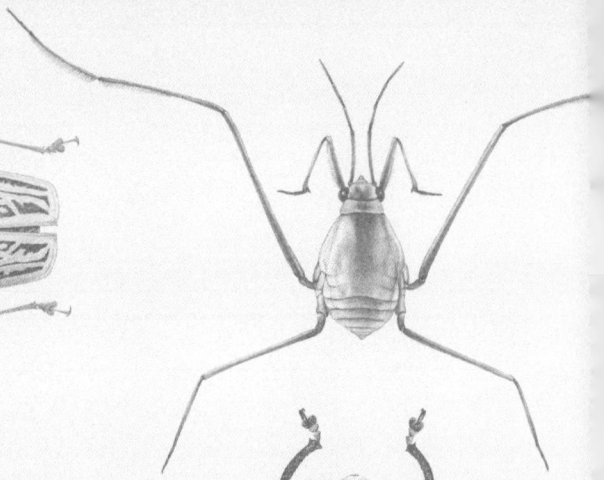

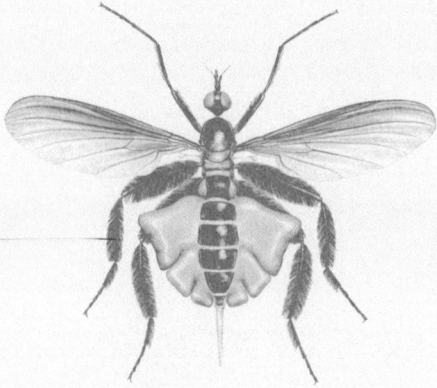

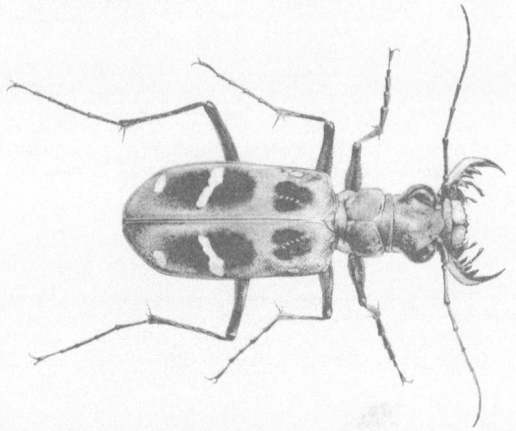

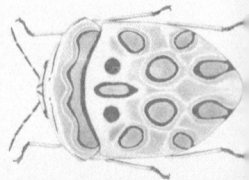